Leader's Guide

to the National Directory *for* Catechesis

Committee on Catechesis

United States Conference of Catholic Bishops
Washington, D.C.

The document *Leader's Guide for the National Directory for Catechesis* was developed as a resource by the Committee on Catechesis of the United States Conference of Catholic Bishops (USCCB). It was reviewed by the committee chairman, Archbishop Daniel M. Buechlein, OSB, and has been authorized for publication by the undersigned.

Msgr. William P. Fay
General Secretary, USCCB

First Printing, July 2005

ISBN 1-57455-695-9

Contents

Resources on CD-ROM

Resources on the CD-ROM include text resource files in Microsoft Word format and slides in Microsoft® PowerPoint® format.

FOUNDATIONAL SESSIONS

Session I—Introduction and Overview of the National Directory for Catechesis

(Slide session in PowerPoint. English and Spanish. *Please note that Session I is based on the* Summary of the National Directory for Catechesis, *which is included in the Leader's Guide book (pp. 43-76) and can be used as an outline for the session.)*

Session II—The Characteristics of Catechesis

(Text resource file in Microsoft Word and slide session in PowerPoint. English and Spanish.)

Session III—Assessing the Present Reality in the Diocese, Parish, or School

(Slide session in PowerPoint. English and Spanish.)

THEMATIC SESSIONS—GOING DEEPER

Methodology

(Text resource file in Microsoft Word and slide session in PowerPoint)

Evangelization

(Text resource file in Microsoft Word and slide session in PowerPoint)

Life in Christ

(Text resource file in Microsoft Word and slide session in PowerPoint)

Sacraments

(Text resource file in Microsoft Word and slide session in PowerPoint)

Prayer and Popular Devotions

(Text resource file in Microsoft Word and slide session in PowerPoint)

Parents and Family

(Text resource file in Microsoft Word and slide session in PowerPoint)

Ecumenical

(Text resource file in Microsoft Word and slide session in PowerPoint)

Lifelong Learning

(Text resource file in Microsoft Word and slide session in PowerPoint)

Organizing Ministry

(Text resource file in Microsoft Word and slide session in PowerPoint)

Those Who Catechize

(Text resource file in Microsoft Word and slide session in PowerPoint)

SUPPLEMENTAL MATERIALS

Talks from the January Symposium on the *National Directory for Catechesis* (on CD-ROM and available in Spanish at *www.usccb.org/education/ndc/symposium.shtml*)

National Directory for Catechesis Bulletin Insert (on CD-ROM and printed in Leader's Guide. English and Spanish.)

Catechetical Prayer from *Book of Blessings* (on CD-ROM and printed in Leader's Guide)

Electronic version of pages 3-34 of the *Leader's Guide to the National Directory for Catechesis* in Adobe Acrobat PDF format (on CD-ROM and printed in Leader's Guide)

Introduction

NOTES ABOUT THE
NATIONAL DIRECTORY FOR CATECHESIS

The *National Directory for Catechesis* (NDC) for the United States of America was approved by the Catholic bishops of the United States in June 2003. The Vatican's *recognitio* of the *Directory* was received December 16, 2004. The NDC was published on May 1, 2005, and took effect on that date. The NDC is approved for use in the Roman Catholic Church and does not apply to Eastern Catholic Churches.

The bishops stated, "the publication of this *National Directory for Catechesis* expresses our continuing pastoral care for catechetical ministry . . . [and] bears witness to our commitment to proclaim the Gospel" (NDC, page 7).

In explaining the purpose of the NDC, the bishops wrote that it is intended as "a source of inspiration for catechesis in the dioceses and parishes of the United States and an important reference point for the formation of catechists and the preparation of catechetical resources":

1. The NDC provides "the fundamental theological and pastoral principles" for catechesis

2. The NDC offers guidelines for applying those principles to catechesis in the United States

3. The NDC sets "forth the nature, purpose, object, tasks, basic content, and various methodologies of catechesis" (Introduction, 5. Purpose of the *Directory*)

The intended audience for the NDC primarily includes those who have responsibility for catechesis in the dioceses, parishes, and schools in the United States.

Here is a brief overview of the content of the NDC by chapter:

- The Introduction establishes the present reality of catechesis.

- Chapter 1 establishes the context in which catechesis occurs.

- Chapter 2 places catechesis within the Church's mission to evangelize.

- Chapter 3 provides the criteria for the authentic presentation of the Christian message.

- Chapter 4 describes God's self-revelation in Christ through the Holy Spirit as the norm for all catechetical methodologies, addresses the human elements of catechetical methodology, and examines the impact of communication technology on the proclamation of the Gospel.

- Chapter 5 describes the relationship between catechesis and liturgy.

- Chapter 6 describes the catechetical principles and guidelines needed for both personal and social moral formation; it addresses the witness to life in Christ to be given by both individuals and communities of faith.

- Chapter 7 describes those involved in the catechetical process and gives principles, guidelines, and criteria for presenting the Gospel to different groups in diverse settings.

- Chapter 8 describes the roles and responsibilities of all who participate in the Church's catechetical mission; it provides principles, guidelines, and criteria for their formation as catechists.

- Chapter 9 describes the various roles and collaboration needed to support the Church's catechetical ministry; it gives the principles, guidelines, and criteria for organizing catechesis.

- Chapter 10 provides the principles, guidelines, and criteria for developing and producing catechetical resources, and for selecting, evaluating, and using those resources.

- The Conclusion offers an expression of enthusiasm and hope for the success of catechesis.

WELCOME TO THE LEADER'S GUIDE

*Go, therefore, and make disciples of all nations, baptizing them in the name of the Father,
and of the Son, and of the holy Spirit, teaching them to observe all that I have commanded you.
And behold, I am with you always, until the end of the age. (Mt 28:19-20)*

This *Leader's Guide to the "National Directory for Catechesis"* (henceforth *Leader's Guide*) is intended for those who are responsible for the implementation of the *National Directory for Catechesis* in dioceses, parishes, and schools. If you are reading this, you might be a member of a diocesan catechetical office, a parish catechetical director, or a school principal or department chair.

The *Leader's Guide* (with its accompanying CD-ROM) does not take the place of reading the NDC, nor is it a commentary or explanation. Rather, it provides you with a set of foundational and thematic sessions with corresponding text resource files and Microsoft® PowerPoint® slides. It is designed to help leaders who have read and understood the NDC to present it to others. While the materials offered here will help you and other catechetical leaders introduce the NDC to many different audiences, only your close and careful reading of the NDC itself will prepare you to teach the document. In addition, while the sessions derived from these materials will help your participants to understand the NDC, the sessions do not replace their own careful reading and studying of the document. Encourage participants to bring their own copies of the NDC with them in order to derive the most benefit from the sessions.

The CD-ROM that accompanies this *Leader's Guide* contains three foundational sessions and ten thematic sessions in PowerPoint slide format. In the three foundational sessions, Session I includes an introduction and overview (based on the *Summary of the "National Directory for Catechesis"*) that is designed to introduce a general audience to the contents of the NDC in a brief amount of time; Foundational Session II focuses on the characteristics of catechesis that weave throughout the NDC and lays the groundwork for Session III; and Session III is an assessment that leads participants through a process to assess their present reality in light of the content and context of the NDC. The foundational sessions are followed by ten thematic sessions that present the NDC in more detail.

The CD-ROM also includes ten Microsoft Word® text resource files that correspond to the ten thematic sessions. These can be used to create outlines, scripts, slides, or new material. The text resource files are designed to keep the key points to remember about the NDC in front of the facilitator as he/she facilitates the session. They highlight key elements from the *National Directory*, and note the key resources available.

The *Summary of the "National Directory for Catechesis"* is included in this printed *Leader's Guide* and also in PowerPoint format (Session I: *Introduction and Overview of the "National Directory for Catechesis"*) and Microsoft Word format on the CD-ROM. The content of the materials is taken from the NDC or consists of summary statements of NDC materials.

Technical Notes

In order to use the PowerPoint files, you will need a computer equipped with a CD-ROM drive and the PowerPoint software. In order to show the PowerPoint files during a session, you will also need an LCD projector and a computer. If an LCD projector is not available, the PowerPoint files can be printed in order to create overheads or handouts to distribute to participants. In order to use the text resource files, you will need a computer equipped with a CD-ROM drive and Microsoft® Word® software.

Guidelines
for Sessions

ROLES AND RESPONSIBILITIES

For both Foundational and Thematic Sessions

Host and Facilitator

General Responsibilities: The **host** schedules the sessions, provides hospitality, and prepares the prayer. The **facilitator** is intimately familiar with the contents of the *National Directory for Catechesis* (NDC) and the session outlines and has prepared the sessions. The host and facilitator can be the same person.

Host's Specific Responsibilities

- Schedule the date, time, and place for the session.

- Publicize the date and time of the session using available means, e.g., parish bulletin, direct mailing, announcements at mass.

- Plan, gather, and set up refreshments for breaks and meals. Solicit volunteers to assist with meals, if needed.

- Prepare and lead prayer at the beginning and end of the session. If time allows, identify prayers or music that can be used at various times throughout the session, especially to gather the group following a break.

- Gather all materials needed for prayer before the session, including music editions, handouts, candles, and tape or CD player.

- Decide how to welcome the participants. Does this group need nametags? Do these participants need an exercise to help them introduce themselves to the group? Gather any materials needed for the welcome and introduction of participants.

- Distribute schedules and handouts.

- Introduce the guest facilitator, if any.

- Coordinate clean-up after the session.

- Coordinate any follow-up with the participants and facilitator (if applicable) after the session.

Facilitator's Specific Responsibilities

- Explain the purpose, format, intended outcome, and structure of the session. Most of this information is provided under "Description of Sessions" (see pp. 14 and 34).

- Give an overview of the material to be explored during the session.

- Establish small groups, if needed.

- If appropriate, review and address questions on material from any previous session(s).

- Lead the presentation using the session outlines from this book, the PowerPoint slides from the CD-ROM, and/or the Word resource files from the CD-ROM. For the thematic sessions, review the "Points to Remember about the NDC" with the participants (see text resource files on CD for each individual session).

- Invite questions and discussion after each subsection of the presentation as needed. Possible questions include the following:

  - What key points from the NDC were presented in this session?

  - From today's discussion, what can be applied to your particular ministry?

  - What one or two new things have you learned about the *National Directory for Catechesis* during this session?

  - How will this new learning affect your ministry or work, or affect the parish as an evangelizing and catechizing community?

  - In what ways has your work been affirmed during this workshop?

  - What next steps are suggested from today's session?

- Encourage the participants to make connections between the content of the session and their ministry in the diocese, parish, or school.

- Oversee small group discussions. Develop discussion and application questions.

- End the session with a quick review of the material that has been presented.

- If additional sessions are planned, assign reading homework and offer reflection questions to be considered before the next session.

- Facilitate any additional large group discussion on the changes that participants expect from the implementation of the NDC, and explore what continued support they need in order to be a catalyst for change.

- Explain what steps are in place for implementing the NDC in the diocese, parish, or school. Ask for suggestions on how this could be done more effectively.

- Ask for final comments or questions.

- Lead the session evaluation.

STRUCTURING SESSIONS

When planning any of the sessions, keep the following suggestions in mind.

1. Begin every session with prayer.

- Include in each prayer a reading and reflection on Sacred Scripture. Use the Scripture passage at the beginning of any chapter of the NDC. There are also prayers used throughout this leader's guide.

- Use the Liturgy of the Hours, part of the Church's tradition, as a source for prayer.

2. Focus on Evangelization. The focus of the *National Directory for Catechesis* (NDC) is on evangelization.

- The purpose of the New Evangelization is to bring about faith and conversion to Christ in all people.

- Those who proclaim the Christian message must know and love the culture and the people to whom they bring the message in order to transform it and the people and make them new in Christ.

- The New Evangelization demands both the inculturation of the Gospel and the transformation of the culture by the Gospel.

- Evangelization within the United States must take into consideration the great diversity of the country, along with all of the cultural challenges present.

3. Keep the General Directory for Catechesis and the Catechism of the Catholic Church at Hand.

- The NDC builds upon the Church's catechetical documents developed during and since the Second Vatican Council. The catechetical vision presented in the NDC comes mostly from the *General Directory for Catechesis* (GDC), while the doctrinal content comes primarily from the *Catechism of the Catholic Church* (CCC). Help participants to see this connection.

- The video *Seeds of Promise, Seeds of Faith* (produced by the USCCB in collaboration with RCL, 2001) presents the key themes of the GDC and would be a valuable resource in NDC sessions. (For ordering information, please see "Resources Needed" on p. 76.)

4. Plan for Success.

- The materials in this *Leader's Guide* and its accompanying CD-ROM provide the background information for all sessions.

- Foundational Sessions: The *Leader's Guide* includes detailed outlines for Sessions II and III that can be adapted as needed by the facilitator.

- As facilitator, you will need to be familiar with the NDC and the session outlines and then must decide how best to engage the participants in the learning process. Some questions for you to consider:

  - How much material can we cover before a break is needed?
  - When will small and large group discussions be most effective?
  - How will we use the PowerPoint sessions?

- Will handouts of the sessions be prepared for people to use for note-taking? (PowerPoint slides can be printed for handouts. In addition, Foundational Sessions II and III include handouts.)
- What types of discussion questions will be needed for each topic or section of the session? (You or the facilitator will have to develop these questions.)

■ Set realistic goals for each session based upon the participants who will be present and the content to be covered.

■ Develop a schedule for each session and give it to participants.

■ For sessions longer than 60 minutes, incorporate breaks.

■ Have enough copies of handouts and of the *Summary* and/or the *National Directory for Catechesis* for each person who attends.

5. Know the Audience.

Those attending the sessions should be adults. Although the NDC guides catechetical formation for all people, including children, it recognizes that the catechetical formation of adults is the principal form of catechesis. Consider these guidelines of adult catechesis:

■ Treat adults as adults, respecting their knowledge and experience.

■ Engage them in conversation.

■ Invite them to make connections between the content and their ministry or life experience.

■ Allow time during the session for group discussion and interaction between the group and the facilitator.

6. Treat the NDC as a Whole Document.

■ The NDC is divided into an Introduction, ten chapters, and a Conclusion. Every chapter of the NDC builds upon, interacts with, and is understood in light of the one that precedes it.

- Every chapter is equally important.
- Some ideas may be repeated in more than one chapter. This is because an idea will be raised in one chapter and then be addressed again in a later chapter from a different perspective.

■ Foundational Session I covers all twelve sections of the NDC.

■ Each thematic session presents targeted information according to its placement within the structure of the *National Directory for Catechesis*.

- Just as no chapter can stand apart from the entire NDC, no theme can be fully understood in isolation from the other themes presented in the NDC.
- One must understand the culture of those being catechized (Chapter 1) before he or she can introduce the faith of the Church to them (Chapter 3), celebrate that faith as a worshiping community (Chapter 5), prepare them for a moral life in Christ (Chapter 6), organize catechetical ministry for them (Chapter 9), or develop resources (Chapter 10) that will serve them well.

■ Because of this repetition of ideas throughout the chapters, every thematic session should begin with the "Points to Remember About the NDC" and then address the theme being discussed.

■ Foundational Sessions II and III trace how the characteristics of catechesis are woven throughout the NDC, showing how no one chapter fully addresses each characteristic.

■ The facilitator's challenge during the sessions is to keep calling people back to the entire document.

7. Model Effective Catechetical Methods.

■ When presenting, adapting, or modifying any of the sessions, model the different catechetical methods that work most effectively with and for adults. The NDC calls for a harmony between the content and method of catechesis. This same balance should be seen in the presentations of the Foundational and Thematic Sessions. The facilitator should:

• Engage the participants in discussion. Challenge them not only to understand, but also to accept and integrate what is being taught.
• Have them work together in small groups to develop practical applications for their particular settings.
• Encourage questions, and seek answers from the group

■ Use the PowerPoint presentations effectively.

• PowerPoint presentations are an effective way to communicate large amounts of information succinctly.
• The facilitator plays a key role in helping the participants understand and integrate new behaviors and knowledge.
• The facilitator guides the learners through the session, rather than serving as an expert telling the participants about the NDC or catechesis.
• When indicated or when possible, the facilitator invites the participants into a dialogue.

8. Evaluate the Effectiveness of the Session.

■ Evaluations help facilitators understand both what people learned and whether the intended outcome was accomplished.

■ Modify the evaluation as needed based on the particular content and outcome of the sessions. That is, because the topic for each session will be different, the evaluation for each will be different as well.

■ Prepare a printed evaluation with a few basic questions on it to distribute to participants. Ask three sets of questions:

1. Questions concerning the setting. (These questions should be asked early in the session as well as on the evaluation form at the conclusion of the session.)
   • Could the facilitator be seen and heard?
   • Could the projections be seen?
   • Could the facilitator be clearly understood?

2. Questions concerning how the content was understood.
   • What did participants learn?
   • What did they find helpful?
   • What was not helpful?
   • What local impact do they anticipate will come out of what they have learned?

3. Questions to determine what further information is needed to implement the NDC locally.
   • Following the session, review the written evaluations.
     • Questions about settings—adjust the setting as needed for any subsequent sessions.
     • Questions about outcomes—determine if the outcome was accomplished. If not, identify what can be done to supplement the session in order to achieve the intended outcome.
     • Questions about further information—note what additional information the participants needed. Identify ways to provide the information and support the implementation of the NDC.

Foundational Sessions

SAMPLE SCHEDULES FOR FOUNDATIONAL SESSIONS

The Foundational Sessions provided in this *Leader's Guide* may be conducted in one or multiple sessions. The following are suggestions for various timeframes.

Schedule for a Single-Day Event

Session I: Introduction and Overview of the *National Directory for Catechesis* (90 minutes)

Break (15 minutes)

Session II: The Characteristics of Catechesis (90 minutes)

Lunch (30-45 minutes)

Session III: Assessing the Present Reality in the Diocese, Parish, or School (2 hours)

Schedule for Two Sessions

This schedule is for two sessions that would be held on consecutive days or weeks.

First Day

Session I: Introduction and Overview of the *National Directory for Catechesis* (90 minutes)

Break (15 minutes)

Session II: The Characteristics of Catechesis (90 minutes)

Preparation for Next Day or Week (15 minutes)

Second Day

Review of Sessions I and II (15 minutes)

Session III: Assessing the Present Reality in the Diocese, Parish, or School (2 hours)

Wrap-Up of All Three Sessions (15 minutes)

Schedule for Three Sessions

This schedule is for sessions that would be held on consecutive days or weeks.

First Day

Session I: Introduction and Overview of the *National Directory for Catechesis* (90 minutes)

Preparation for Next Day or Week (15 minutes)

Second Day

Review of Session I (15 minutes)

Session II: The Characteristics of Catechesis (90 minutes)

Preparation for Next Day or Week (15 minutes)

Third Day

Review of Session I and II (15 minutes)

Session III: Assessing the Present Reality in the Diocese, Parish, or School (2 hours)

Wrap-Up of All Three Sessions (15 minutes)

DESCRIPTION OF FOUNDATIONAL SESSIONS

The three foundational sessions are designed to be used together to provide a comprehensive overview of the *National Directory for Catechesis* (NDC) and its implications for catechetical ministry within specific communities.

Session I: Introduction and Overview of the National Directory for Catechesis

Session I offers a summary look at the contents of each chapter of the NDC.

Intended Outcome: Participants gain a general understanding of the NDC and how it affects both catechetical ministry and their own ministries.

Purpose: Designed to be used as a one-session, general introduction to the NDC. This is the first part of a three-part program on the foundations of catechesis. Possible settings:

- A talk during a diocesan catechetical day

- A parish education or catechetical committee

- A school in-service, staff meeting, or board meeting

- The first session in a multi-part training day for diocesan, parish, or school leaders

- The initial step in an implementation plan to introduce catechists, teachers, catechetical leaders, principals, and diocesan staff members to the NDC

Intended Audience: Members and leaders of diocesan, parish, and schools staffs who participate in any way in catechetical ministry; diocesan, parish, and school education and catechetical commissions and committees; parishioners engaged in ministries related to catechesis; and the general parish population.

Time: 90 to 120 minutes

CD-ROM Materials: *Introduction and Overview of the National Directory for Catechesis* (PowerPoint).

Suggested Resources: While participants do not need a copy of the NDC for this session, they will benefit from having a printed copy of the *Summary of the National Directory for Catechesis*. You may also wish to distribute copies of the *National Directory for Catechesis Bulletin Insert*. (For ordering information, please see "Resources Needed" on p. 36)

Session II: The Characteristics of Catechesis

Session II leads the participants through an overview of the characteristics of catechesis and how they are implemented in the diocese, parish, or school.

Intended Outcome: Participants clearly articulate the characteristics of catechesis and identify the challenges of the characteristics for their particular community.

Purpose: Designed to be used as the second part of a three-part program on the foundations of catechesis. Possible settings:

- A diocesan catechetical day

- A teacher in-service or staff meeting

- A parish education or catechetical committee

- A one session in a multi-day or evening training session in dioceses, parishes, and schools

- The initial step in a diocesan, parish, or school implementation plan

Intended Audience: Members and leaders of diocesan, parish, and school staffs who participate in any way in catechetical ministry; diocesan, parish, and school education and catechetical commissions and committees; parishioners engaged in ministries related to catechesis; and the general parish population.

Time: 90 minutes

CD-ROM Materials: *The Characteristics of Catechesis* (PowerPoint); *The Characteristics of Catechesis* (resource file in Word).

Suggested Resources: Participants will benefit from having a printed copy of the *Summary of the National Directory for Catechesis* during the session. You may also wish to make available copies of the *National Directory for Catechesis*. (For ordering information, please see "Resources Needed" on p. 36.)

Session III: Assessing the Present Reality in the Diocese, Parish, or School

Session III leads the participants through an assessment of the diocesan, parish, or school catechetical program. The characteristics of catechesis from Session II are the basis for the assessment.

Intended Outcome: Participants assess their basic understanding of six key characteristics of catechesis; identify strengths and areas for growth for the diocesan, parish, or school catechetical ministry; name opportunities for and threats to growth in the diocesan, parish, or school catechetical ministry; and create strategies to improve the diocesan, parish, or school catechetical ministry.

Purpose: Designed to be used as the third part of a three-part program on the NDC. Possible settings:

■ A diocesan catechetical day

■ A teacher in-service or staff meeting

■ A parish education or catechetical committee

■ A one session in a multi-day or evening training session in dioceses, parishes, and schools

■ The initial step in a diocesan, parish, or school implementation plan

Intended Audience: Members and leaders of diocesan, parish, and schools staffs who participate in any way in catechetical ministry; diocesan, parish, and school education and catechetical commissions and committees; parishioners engaged in ministries related to catechesis; and the general parish population.

Time: 120 minutes

CD-ROM Materials: *Assessing the Present Reality in the Diocese, Parish, or School* (PowerPoint).

Suggested Resources: Participants will benefit from having a printed copy of the *Summary of the National Directory for Catechesis* during the session. You may also wish to make copies of the *National Directory for Catechesis* available. (For ordering information, please see "Resources Needed" on p. 36.)

FOUNDATIONAL SESSION OUTLINES

Materials Needed

- Bible

- Nametags, one per participant

- Newsprint, a dry-erase board, or a chalkboard

- Markers or chalk

- *National Directory for Catechesis*, one per participant

- *Summary of the National Directory for Catechesis*, one per participant

Session I—Introduction and Overview of the National Directory for Catechesis

Please note that Session I is based on the *Summary of the National Directory for Catechesis*, which is included in this book (pp. 43-76). The structure of the *Summary* can be used as an outline for the session. For general suggestions for formatting the session, see the Suggested Schedule Outline for Thematic Sessions (p. 32).

Session II—Characteristics of Catechesis

Preparation

Make sufficient copies of Handouts 1 and 2 (pp. 19-22), one for each participant.

Welcome (5 minutes)

Gather the session participants in the meeting space. Take a few minutes to introduce all of the participants. If the group is large or unfamiliar to each other, invite the participants to create nametags.

Opening Prayer and Reflection (10 minutes)

Read Matthew 28:19-20.

Invite the participants to share their reflections on the Gospel and to respond to the following questions. If the participants are formed into small groups or pairs, encourage them to share their comments with the large group at the end of the time.

1. What are the challenges in Jesus' commands? How do Jesus' commands challenge our community to grow?

2. What promise does Jesus make to his disciples? Where do we see signs of that promise in our own community?

Characteristics of Catechesis: Our Community's Understanding (20 minutes)

List the two open-ended statements below on newsprint, a chalkboard, or a dry-erase board. Distribute blank paper and pencils or pens. Ask all of the participants to respond, individually at first, to the two open-ended statements using the paper provided to write down their answers.

1. Catechesis is . . .

2. The key characteristics of catechesis are . . .

Invite the participants to share their responses with one or two people near them. Re-gather the group, and solicit the responses to the statements. List the responses on newsprint, a dry-erase board, or a chalkboard, highlighting those that are repeated or receive strong support.

Share the following description of catechesis with the group using Slides 2-4 of the PowerPoint presentation. Ask the participants if they want to add or modify any of their previous responses.

Catechesis . . .

- Describes the many ways in which the teachings of Christ have been passed on to believers since the beginning of the Church

- Is an essential mission of the Church

- Helps people come to know about God with the hope that, in knowing him, they may want to enter into relationship with him and desire to be transformed by him

- Is a right of the baptized person

- Is the means to fulfill the baptized person's corresponding responsibility to continue to grow in knowledge and love of God

Review the responses, and then ask the group to state in one or two sentences their response to this question: "As we look at our set of definitions and characteristics for catechesis, what are the primary characteristics of catechesis in our parish (or diocese)?" List the characteristics on newsprint, a dry-erase board, or a chalkboard. Combine and refine the list until the group arrives at one list of characteristics that they can support.

Characteristics of Catechesis (20 minutes)

Present Slides 5-28 of the PowerPoint presentation on the "Characteristics of Catechesis." Use the backgrounder on the CD-ROM for more detailed information.

In small groups of three people, complete Handout 1, identifying key words or phrases for the characteristics of catechesis.

Key Words/Phrases for Characteristics of Catechesis

Characteristics	Key Words or Phrases
Authentic	
Complete	
Systematic	
Integral	
Divine Pedagogy	
Lifelong	
Inculturated	

Formulate a cohesive statement for the characteristics of catechesis using the key words or phrases.

In the large group, share the small groups' lists, refining them to arrive at a large-group statement of the characteristics of catechesis.

Distribute copies of Handout 2, "Characteristics of Catechesis." (Key words and phrases are highlighted for easy reference by the facilitator and participants.) Review the characteristics that were described in the PowerPoint presentation and listed on Handout 2. Ask for any modifications or additions to the large-group statement that was developed in the previous step.

The Church teaches that catechesis should have the following characteristics.

I. Authentic catechesis

- **Faithfully teaches the doctrine and traditions of the Catholic Church,** which are safeguarded by the bishops, who teach with a unique authority
- Has **Scripture and Tradition** as its **single source** for the Christian message
- Is **centered in Christ**
- Is **trinitarian** in nature and content
- **Comes from and leads to the Church**
- Is **sacramental**
- Focuses on the **moral life**
- Focuses on **eternal life**

A. Catechesis centered in Christ teaches that

- Jesus Christ, the only Son of the Father, **became man.**
- He assumed **human nature** without losing his divine nature.
- Jesus Christ is **true God and true man.**
- All of Christ's life is a teaching.
- He taught in his **words, parables, miracles, prayers, love for people, and acceptance of the will** of his Father, which resulted in the **sacrifice of the cross and the Resurrection.**
- The object of catechesis that is Christ-centered is communion **with Christ.**
- Jesus became man not only so that we might know God's loving **plan for our salvation,** but also that we might **be redeemed through** his life, death, **Resurrection, and glorious Ascension.**

B. Catechesis should be trinitarian in nature and content and teach that

- Trinity is the **central mystery** of the Christian faith and life.
- Through Jesus, the Trinity has been **revealed as God the Father, God the Son, and God the Holy Spirit.**
- Authentic catechesis teaches faithfully what Jesus has revealed.
- The **three divine persons are inseparable** in who they are and in what they do. Yet each is revealed through actions that are proper to him: the Father is revealed through creation, the Son through his redemptive mission, and the Holy Spirit through his sanctifying activity that continues in the Church.
- When **baptized** in the name of the Father, the Son, and the Holy Spirit, we are called to **share in the life of the Blessed Trinity** here on earth and after death for eternity.

C. Catechesis comes from and leads to the Church and teaches that

- **The Church is founded by Jesus Christ** and **guided by the Holy Spirit.**
- The best way to deepen faith is to grow in knowledge of the faith, prepare to receive and celebrate the sacraments, live moral lives, be people of prayer, and witness to Jesus Christ—even in a society that does not always reflect and support Christian values.
- All the baptized are called to **accept the missionary mandate** Christ gave to his disciples to teach in his name.
- Some have **unique responsibilities for catechesis** in the Church: bishops, priests, deacons, consecrated men and women, lay leaders, and parents.
- **Bishops,** as successors of the apostles, are the primary teachers of the Church and receive from Christ the power to act in his name.
- **Parents** are the first and most influential catechists for their children.
- All the baptized who are committed to spreading the Gospel message have a role in the Church's catechetical mission.
- Those who catechize have a unique opportunity to prepare others to witness to Christ in society.

- We firmly believe and hope that after death the righteous will live **forever with the risen Christ.**
- Jesus, the Son of God, **freely suffered death** because of his free and complete acceptance of the Father's will.
- **By his death, Christ conquered death,** and so opened the **possibility of salvation to all.**

II. Complete and systematic catechesis

A. Complete catechesis

- **Reflects the entirety of the teaching of the Church** as found in the *Catechism of the Catholic Church* (1994).
- **Presents the doctrines of the faith as an integrated whole.**
- **Presents the complete content of the *Catechism of the Catholic Church.***
- Includes: the articles of the Creed, the **Seven Sacraments, the Ten Commandments,** and the **petitions of the Lord's Prayer.**
- Has content **rooted in Scripture** and **reflects various sources** of the faith such as the teachings from the Councils, the Eastern and Western Fathers, liturgical texts, and spiritual writings.
- By following the teaching office of the Church, the **Magisterium,** ensures that what the Church teaches in matters of faith and morals is faithful to the teaching of Christ as handed down to us from the Apostles.

B. Systematic catechesis asserts that

- The basic teachings of the faith as found in the *Catechism of the Catholic Church* need to **be taught in a planned manner and be continually reinforced.**
- The teachings of the faith are **expanded upon and adapted** to the age and ability of the learner.
- Instruction in the faith **begins in the home.**
- As the child ages, others support parents in educating their child in the faith by providing **systematic catechetical programs.**

D. Catechesis is sacramental:

- All the liturgy and worship of the Church is catechetical.
- The liturgical life of the Church **revolves around the sacraments** with the **Eucharist at the center.**
- Catechesis communicates sound sacramental theology.
- The sacraments are **efficacious signs of grace instituted by Christ and entrusted to the Church.**
- The Seven Sacraments are **moments of encounter with Christ.**
- Sacramental catechesis is a **comprehensive and systematic formation** in the faith that integrates the knowledge of the faith with the living of the faith.
- Preparation to celebrate and receive the sacraments is intended for all members of the Church.
- The sacramental life of the Church takes place within and involves the community of faith.
- Sacramental catechesis is **lifelong and ongoing.**

E. Catechesis focuses on the moral life:

- It **prepares believers to be disciples of Jesus Christ,** that is, to have complete life in Christ.
- It stirs the heart, enlightens the mind, and inspires the soul.
- It seeks to help people **form correct consciences, choose what is morally good, avoid sin, and live in this world** according to the prompting of the Holy Spirit.
- It teaches what it means to live according to the moral teachings of the Church, especially as found in the **moral law or Ten Commandments,** presented **in light of Christ's teaching in the Sermon on the Mount.**

F. Catechesis focuses on eternal life and teaches us that

- We should look beyond this life to salvation and eternal life with God.
- The **Creed is our profession of faith** in God: Father, Son, and Holy Spirit.

- Programs of **adult faith formation in the RCIA process** should include systematic catechesis.
- Catechesis is to be a **lifelong and ongoing catechetical activity.**
- A **variety of methods and techniques** can be employed in the transmission of the knowledge of the faith. "Learning 'by heart'" (memorization) is particularly important.
- **What is to be memorized** includes prayers, facts about Scripture, key themes and major figures in salvation history, facts about the Church, worship and the Church year, devotions, holy days, the saints, the works of mercy, the mysteries of the Rosary, the Stations of the Cross, the Ten Commandments, the Beatitudes, the Gifts and Fruits of the Holy Spirit, theological and moral virtues, Precepts of the Church, principles of Catholic social teaching, the examination of conscience, and songs.

III. *Integral Catechesis*

- All the teachings of the Church are **interrelated and complement one another.**
- The teachings **form an organic whole** because there is only one source for catechesis, the Word of God revealed by Jesus Christ.
- All catechesis draws its content from this one source as transmitted **through Scripture and Tradition.**
- There **are no contradictions;** all the teachings **support and uphold** one another.

IV. *Divine Pedagogy*

- What we believe and teach has **first been taught to us by God.**
- The **content** of our faith has been **revealed to us by him and transmitted through Scripture and Tradition.**
- All of what we teach comes to us from God through the Church.

- We teach about the **very nature of the God who loves us** and who wants to effect in us a **response to this love: a conversion to Christ** that leads to faith that is celebrated, lived, and prayed.

V. *Lifelong catechesis*

- Catechesis should be a **permanent part of our lives.**
- Catechists should be **formed and trained** to teach the Gospel message according to their particular circumstances.
- **Catechetical materials** are to be **carefully selected** so that the faith can be taught in such a way that the person **can incorporate the doctrine according to his or her age and ability.**
- We **never learn** all we can or need to know.
- **Ongoing catechesis** ensures continuing **conversion to Christ** and living lives compatible with the Gospel.

VI. *Inculturated catechesis*

- Catechesis must **reflect an understanding of the culture** in which the learner lives and how the Gospel message can transform the culture. This is one aspect of the meaning of **inculturation.**
- Inculturation involves **identifying the presence of God and traces of the Gospel message in a culture** and discerning how the Gospel message can be brought effectively to the people of that culture.
- A catechesis of inculturation means presenting the teaching of the faith in a **complete and authentic way in dialogue with the language, customs, and practices** of those to whom the Gospel is presented.
- The **cultural pluralism** in the United States is a positive value.
- **Distinct cultural identities** should be preserved while the unity of faith is promoted.

Promoting the Characteristics of Catechesis (30 minutes)

Write the words "Similarities" and "Differences" on two sheets of newsprint or in two separate columns on a dry-erase board or chalkboard. Lead a discussion of the differences and similarities between the two lists of the characteristics of catechesis. Highlight in some way (e.g., circle or underline words or phrases in different colors) the similarities and differences in the lists posted in front of the group.

Using the information from the presentation and discussion, invite the participants to create a list of ideas that respond to the questions below. Use Slides 29-31 of the PowerPoint presentation to display the questions.

1. What characteristics of catechesis in this parish (or diocese) are affirmed? What aspects need to be challenged?

2. In what ways is our parish (or diocese) well equipped to meet these challenges? In what ways do we need to grow?

3. What opportunities do the characteristics of catechesis create for our parish (or diocese)?

4. What resources (e.g., staff, money, facilities, material, volunteers) do we have that could make the characteristics of catechesis a fuller reality in our parish (or diocese)?

5. What are the first three steps that we want to take to make the characteristics of catechesis a fuller reality in our parish (or diocese)?

Closing Prayer (5 minutes)

(The text of the prayer is also available on Slide 32 of the PowerPoint presentation.)

Prayer to Mary, Star of Evangelization
O Blessed Virgin Mary,
we ask you who prayed to strengthen the faith of the first disciples
to obtain for the Church in the United States an outpouring of the Holy Spirit,
to guide us in a new evangelization.
Help us teach the faith in such a way that the members of the Church today
will truly be Christ's disciples of this new millennium,
drawing people throughout the world to the saving message and power of Christ.
We ask this through Jesus Christ, your Son and our Lord. Amen

Mary, Star of Evangelization, pray for us.

Adapted from the *National Directory for Catechesis*, p. 302.

Session III—Assessing the Present Reality in the Diocese, Parish, or School

Preparation

Before the assessment, determine what area or aspect of catechetical ministry this session will cover—e.g., catechesis for children, youth, or adults. If the assessment is going to cover all catechesis, include a small group of people who have specific knowledge about that area of catechesis in the parish. Ask them to draw upon their area-specific experience and knowledge as they respond to the assessment questions.

Welcome (5 minutes)

Gather the session participants in the meeting space. Take a few minutes to introduce all of the participants. If the group is large or unfamiliar to each other, invite the participants to create nametags.

Opening Prayer and Reflection (15 minutes)

Read Matthew 13:52. Invite the participants to share their reflections on the Gospel passage and to respond to the following questions. If the participants are formed into small groups or pairs, encourage them to share their comments with the large group at the end of the time.

1. In what ways are we like the head of the household in the Gospel?

2. What responsibilities do we bear as the "heads" of our catechetical ministry?

3. How does a responsible "head of household" decide which old and new elements to bring out from the catechetical "storeroom"?

4. What are some of the old and new elements of our catechetical ministry that we need to discuss today?

Conclude with a prayer, asking God to keep us open-minded as we look at the present and future of our catechetical ministry.

Defining Our Terms (15-25 minutes)

The success of assessing our work and programs can be improved if we share the same definitions of rich, complex, and meaningful words.

With the large group, define the word "catechesis." Compare the group's understanding of catechesis with the definition below. Show slides 2-3 of the Session III PowerPoint presentation that lists the definition of "catechesis." The text of those slides follows.

(If the participants have completed Session II, note that this is a review of the material covered in that session.)

Catechesis . . .

- Describes the many ways in which the teachings of Christ have been passed on to believers since the beginning of the Church.

- Is an essential mission of the Church.

- Helps people come to know about God with the hope that, in knowing him, they will want to enter into relationship with him and desire to be transformed by him.

- Is a right of the baptized person.

- Is the means to fulfill the baptized person's corresponding responsibility to continue to grow in their knowledge and love of God.

Based on these statements about catechesis, ask the group whether and how they want to modify their definition of catechesis.

Form the participants into pairs. Ask them to define or describe the characteristics of catechesis using Handout 1 from Session II (pg. 19). Give them 10 minutes for this task.

(If the participants have previously completed Session II, especially on the same day, review Handout 2, "Characteristics of Catechesis" [pp. 20-22], on the characteristics of catechesis. Then skip to the next section, "Strengths of Our Catechetical Programs.")

In the large group, invite the participants to share their definitions or descriptions. List the responses from the pairs on newsprint, a dry-erase board, or a chalkboard. Distribute copies of Handout 2 from Session II (pp. 20-22). Using Handout 2, compare the definitions or descriptions of the participants with those from the *National Directory for Catechesis*. If time permits, ask the participants to refine their definitions or descriptions to incorporate any new information or insight from the large group discussion. Post the final versions of the definitions or descriptions in the room.

Strengths of Our Catechetical Programs (30 minutes)
Working in groups of three to five people, ask the participants to complete Handout 3 on the next page, "Strengths of Our Catechetical Program." Allow 15 minutes. (Slide 4 from the Session III PowerPoint presentation also contains the information on Handout 3.)

When the groups have completed Handout 3, continue with the next set of directions.

Handout 3

Directions: For each characteristic of catechesis, identify up to five examples to evaluate the effectiveness of your catechetical program.

Is it authentic?

Is it complete?

Is it systematic?

Is it integral?

Does it highlight divine pedagogy?

Is it lifelong?

Is it inculturated?

Ask each group to assign a number to all of their examples using the following assessment scale. Show Slide 5 of the PowerPoint presentation, which also contains the assessment scale.

3 = We do this consistently well. No improvement is needed.

2 = We do this well. We need to continue to improve on this.

1 = We do this better now than in the past, but it continues to be an area of challenge and growth for us.

Gather all of the participants into a large group. Ask the small groups to share their examples, for each characteristic, that received a rating of "3." Using newsprint, a dry-erase board, or a chalkboard, list the responses, categorized by characteristic. Ask if any of the groups rated any of the examples differently. Inquire about the differences, then ask the group as a whole to assign a number to the example. Put that example on the appropriate list.

Affirm the participants, especially those who are directly responsible for leading and implementing any of the examples that received a "3."

Do the same process for the examples that received a "2" and a "1." For the "2s," ask the group to name one or two actions that could be taken to ensure that improvement continues. Set aside any discussion of the examples that received a rating of "1" until later.

Areas of Growth for Our Catechetical Program (30 minutes)

Returning to the previous small groups, ask the participants to complete Handout 4, "Areas of Growth for Our Catechetical Program." Allow 15 minutes. Slide 6 of the PowerPoint presentation also contains the directions for Handout 4.

When the groups have completed Handout 4, continue with the next set of directions.

Handout 4

Directions: For each characteristic of catechesis, identify up to five examples of how your catechetical program needs to grow in each of the following areas.

Being authentic

Being complete

Being systematic

Being integral

Highlighting divine pedagogy

Being lifelong

Being inculturated

Ask each group to assign a number to all of their examples using the following assessment scale. Show Slide 7, which contains the assessment scale for this step.

−3 = We are very challenged by this. We have not started to address this.

−2 = We are challenged by this. We have taken some limited steps toward addressing this.

−1 = We are challenged by this, but we are starting to think about or work at addressing this.

Gather all of the participants into a large group. Ask the small groups to share their examples receiving a rating of "−1" under each characteristic. Using newsprint, a dry-erase board, or a chalkboard, list the responses, categorized by characteristic. Ask if any of the groups rated any of the examples listed differently. Inquire about the differences, then ask the group as a whole to assign a number ("−1" or something else) to the examples in question. Put that example on the appropriate list.

Put the lists of "areas for growth" that received a "−1" alongside those examples that received a "1" during the discussion of strengths. Note any overlap. Affirm the participants for accepting the responsibility to assist the program to meet its challenges, especially those who are directly responsible for leading and implementing any of the examples that received a "1" or "−1." Ask the group to identify why these continue to be challenges and to brainstorm some next steps.

Repeat the same process for the examples that received a "−2." Ask the group to identify some of the reasons why these examples continue to be a challenge. Invite them to name some next steps. Put the responses on newsprint and post them in the room.

Repeat the same process for the examples that received a "−3." Solicit from the group their thoughts about why these are challenges to the community and why the community has not started to address these areas. Ask the group to prioritize five examples receiving a "−3," in the order of what needs to be addressed most. List the responses on newsprint and post them in the room.

Ask the group to share any examples that they did not rate or any examples that have come to mind during the course of the discussion. List those on newsprint, a chalkboard, or dry-erase board. Encourage the group to discuss these two questions briefly.

1. Why aren't we taking these actions?

2. How do we need to grow in order to be ready and able to take these actions?

Moving Toward a Plan (10 minutes)

Invite the participants to gather in small groups based on the area for which they are responsible. Have the groups review the examples of actions that are displayed on the various lists around the room. Ask the small groups to identify five next action steps for their group's area of responsibility. Show Slide 8 of the PowerPoint presentation, which includes Handout 5.

Next Steps

Handout 5

1.

2.

3.

4.

5.

Ask each group to share their list with the large group.

Closing Prayer (5 minutes)

Lead the group in the following closing prayer or a prayer of commitment. A *Litany of the Way* can be prayed antiphonally, led by the leader, by alternating groups (men and women, or different sides of the room), or in unison. For copies of the prayer cards, see "Resources Needed." (p. 36)

A Litany of the Way
Prayer for the Journey

As Jesus sought the quiet of the desert
Teach us to pray.

As Jesus washed the feet of his disciples
Teach us to love.

As Jesus promised Paradise to the thief on the cross
Teach us to hope.

As Jesus called Peter to walk to him across the water
Teach us to believe.

As the child Jesus sat among the elders in the temple
Teach us to seek answers.

As Jesus in the garden opened his mind and heart to God's will
Teach us to listen.

As Jesus reflected on the Law and the Prophets
Teach us to learn.

As Jesus used parables to reveal the mysteries of the Kingdom
Teach us to teach.

Thematic Sessions

SUGGESTED SCHEDULE OUTLINE FOR THEMATIC SESSIONS

Prayer (5-15 minutes)
- Begin and end with prayer.

- If time allows, pray at various times throughout the session. Singing or playing hymns on tapes or CDs is a good way to reconvene the group following a break.

Welcome and Introduction by Host (10-15 minutes)
- Welcome and introduce the participants.

- Explain the purpose, structure, format, and intended outcome of the session.

- Distribute schedules and handouts.

- Establish small groups, if these are needed for the session.

- Introduce the facilitator (when host and facilitator are the same person, introduce self).

Session (60-120 minutes)
- If this session is a continuation of a previous session, review and take questions on the information from the previous session(s).

- Present PowerPoint slides from the CD-ROM, providing additional commentary from the text resources for the topic.

- Take breaks every 60-75 minutes. If lunch is scheduled, allow adequate time for serving and eating the meal and for a 15-minute break. (Schedule two breaks after lunch, each break occurring after 45 minutes of work.)

- Lead small-group activities, if planned.

Wrap-Up (20-30 minutes)
- Wrap up discussion. Identify the changes that participants expect from the implementation of the *National Directory for Catechesis* (NDC) and what continued support they need in order to be effective.

- If additional sessions are planned, assign reading homework from the NDC and offer reflection questions for participants to consider before the next session.

- Identify additional ways to use the material to implement the NDC. Identify how the diocese, parish, or school is already implementing the material in the presentation.

- Evaluate the session.

- End with prayer.

DESCRIPTION OF THEMATIC SESSIONS—GOING DEEPER

This *Leader's Guide* offers ten thematic sessions geared to help pastoral leaders and catechists delve deeper into the context and content of the *National Directory for Catechesis*. Each thematic session leads participants to a deeper understanding of what the NDC says about a specific area of content.

Intended Outcome: Participants become familiar with what the NDC says about the particular theme being discussed and understand how to apply what they have learned at the local level.

Purpose: The thematic sessions are designed to supplement Foundational Sessions I, II, and III. The thematic sessions complement the three foundational sessions by focusing on particular topics or themes. It is recommended that dioceses, parishes, and schools host the foundational sessions first, then identify the appropriate thematic sessions for the audience. Once suitable thematic sessions are selected, each session can be used in the following ways:

- As a workshop at a diocesan catechetical day

- During a meeting of the parish education or catechetical committee

- As part of a school in-service, staff meeting, or board meeting

Intended Audience: While important to all diocesan and parish catechetical and school leaders, the thematic sessions will also be of special interest to those working in the specific area of ministry that the thematic session addresses. For example, the session on sacraments and Mass can also be of interest to the parish liturgy committee and liturgical ministers.

Time: 60 to 90 minutes

CD-ROM Materials: A PowerPoint slide file that can be used for each session and a corresponding Microsoft Word text resource file containing background material are on the accompanying CD-ROM for each of the following thematic session titles:
- *Methodology*

- *Evangelization*

- *Life in Christ*

- *Sacraments*

- *Prayer and Popular Devotions*

- *Parents and Family*

- *Ecumenical*

- *Lifelong Learning*

- *Organizing Ministry*

- *Those Who Catechize*

Suggested Resources: The session is planned around the specific chapters of the NDC that refer to the content being discussed. Participants will find it helpful to have a copy of either the NDC or the *Summary* at hand.

Closing Comments

The *National Directory for Catechesis* is an important document in the life of the Catholic Church in the United States. It will shape how the Church evangelizes through catechesis for many years to come. The PowerPoint slides and text resource files provided in the *Leader's Guide* CD-ROM were created to help diocesan and parish catechetical leaders bring the NDC to life in the local Church. These resources are tools to be used by skilled local leaders.

Feel free to adapt these materials to meet the needs of the local church. If additional sessions or presentations are needed for groups, or for themes not included in the *Leader's Guide,* feel free to create them. The website *www.usccb.org/education/ndc/* managed by the staff of the USCCB Department of Education, will post additional resources and information concerning the implementation of the NDC. Check this website for more information.

May the Spirit of the Living God continue to guide the catechetical mission of the Catholic Church in the United States.

Resources Needed

NDC RESOURCES

National Directory for Catechesis
English: No. 5-443, 328 pp.
Spanish: No. 5-862, 328 pp. (est.)

Summary of the "National Directory for Catechesis"
English: No. 5-696, 48 pp.
Spanish: No. 5-913, 52 pp.

National Directory for Catechesis Bulletin Insert
English: No. 5-697, 2-panel insert
Spanish: No. 5-914, 2-panel insert

To order these resources or to obtain a copy of the USCCB catalog (please specify the catalog in print or on CD), call toll-free 800-235-8722 Monday through Friday from 9:30 a.m. to 5:00 p.m. Eastern time. Visit us on the web at *www.usccb.org*. Para pedidos en español o catálogos, llame gratis al 800-235-8722 y presione 4 para hablar con un representante del servicio al cliente en español. Para llamadas en el área metropolitana de Washington o fuera de los Estados Unidos, llame al 202-722-8716. Nuestra dirección cibernética en el Internet es *www.usccb.org*.

OTHER USEFUL RESOURCES

Catechism of the Catholic Church (CCC)
Hardcover:
    English: No. 5-109, 920 pp.
    Spanish: No. 5-844, 822 pp.
Paperback:
    English: No. 5-110, 920 pp.
    Spanish: No. 5-828, 822 pp.

General Directory for Catechesis (GDC)
English: No. 5-225, 300 pp.
Spanish: No. 5-226, 300 pp.

Our Hearts Were Burning Within Us: A Pastoral Plan for Adult Faith Formation in the United States

English: No. 5-299, 80 pp.
Spanish: No. 5-811, 80 pp.

Leader's Guide to Our Hearts Were Burning Within Us
English: No. 5-342, 96 pp.
Spanish: No. 5-826, 96 pp.

A Litany of the Way (prayer cards)
English: No. 5-505, packages of 100
Spanish: No. 5-875, packages of 100

Seeds of Promise, Seeds of Faith can be ordered from RCL (Resources for Christian Living)

Supplemental
Materials

NATIONAL DIRECTORY
for CATECHESIS

In December 2004, the Vatican approved the new National Directory for Catechesis, *which was developed by the bishops of the United States. The* National Directory for Catechesis, *which is beginning to circulate throughout this country, provides new energy and sharper focus in catechesis. This brief handout answers some questions that people might be asking about this important book.*

1. What is catechesis?

Catechesis is sharing the teachings of Jesus Christ in such a way that a person comes to know about God, to believe in him and his teachings, to enter into a relationship with God, and to be transformed by him. Catechesis involves teaching about doctrine as well as about the living practice of the faith. Catechizing and being catechized are lifelong responsibilities for every Catholic.

2. Is "catechesis" another word for "teaching"?

Yes and no. While catechesis does involve instruction about God and what he has told us, it also involves helping us to become the type of people the Lord intended us to be when he created us. Through catechesis, we learn more about our faith and also deepen our relationship with God—Father, Son, and Holy Spirit.

3. Is catechesis something that involves just children?

No. While many people think of catechesis only in terms of religious education for children, catechesis is really a lifelong activity for every Catholic. A way of living as well as learning, catechesis helps us to grow in faith and to grow closer to God throughout our entire lives.

4. What is the *National Directory for Catechesis*?

The *National Directory for Catechesis* outlines general principles and guidelines for formal catechesis. It is to be used in conjunction with the *Catechism of the Catholic Church*, another important catechetical text, which serves as the definitive reference for the content of catechesis that is authentic and complete. The *National Directory for Catechesis* follows the *General Directory for Catechesis* released in 1997, which presented catechetical principles and guidelines for the universal Church. The *National Directory for Catechesis* adapts the content of the *General Directory for Catechesis* in such a way as to address the particular catechetical needs of the Church in the United States.

5. Who will use the *National Directory for Catechesis*?

It will be used by those who have responsibility for catechesis. This includes those who oversee catechesis on a diocesan level as well as those actively involved in catechetical activities in parishes and in all levels of Catholic education. The *National Directory for Catechesis* will also be a source of guidance for those who prepare materials used for catechesis. Finally, it will be used by those who want to learn more about the catechetical mission of the Church.

6. What does the *National Directory for Catechesis* say?

The *National Directory for Catechesis* is more than three hundred pages long. It explains the meaning of catechesis, looks at the context in which catechesis occurs in this country, identifies the sources and content of catechesis, and addresses practical issues involved in directing and taking part in catechetical activities.

7. What should I remember about catechesis?

Both the *General Directory for Catechesis* and the new *National Directory for Catechesis* remind us that catechesis involves six basic tasks that must take place if catechesis is to be authentic and complete: (1) to promote knowledge of the faith; (2) to promote meaningful participation in liturgical worship and the sacramental life of the Church; (3) to integrate moral formation into a Christian way of life; (4) to teach Christians how to pray with Christ, in Christ, and in communion with the Church; (5) to initiate the Christian into the life of the local church community and foster active participation in the mission of the Church; (6) and to promote a missionary spirit that prepares Christians to witness to Christ in society.

8. What other major points from the *Directory* should I understand?

Both the *General Directory for Catechesis* and the *National Directory for Catechesis* stress two points worth remembering. First, what we believe as Catholics and teach in catechesis has been taught to us first by God. We need to remember that the content of our faith is not the result of personal judgment or some kind of vote. The doctrine we believe is true and reliable because it comes to us from God. The second point is that catechesis is a lifelong responsibility. We never reach a point where we have learned everything, and at no point can we stop sharing the teaching of Jesus Christ with others.

What is in the *National Directory for Catechesis*?

Here is a brief overview of each chapter.

CHAPTER ONE explores the **context** in which we live and worship in the United States—including particular challenges to catechetical efforts.

CHAPTER TWO explains the **meaning of catechesis** and the various **types of catechesis**. It also explains how catechesis is related to Revelation and to evangelization.

CHAPTER THREE gives an overview of the **content of catechesis**—the truths that have come to us through Revelation as found in Scripture and Tradition.

CHAPTER FOUR presents the **methods** used in catechesis. This includes an understanding of how God has taught us, as well as the various human methodologies that can and should be employed to continue this teaching.

CHAPTER FIVE focuses on **liturgy**. Every liturgy is catechetical because we learn about aspects of our faith through prayer and sacramental celebrations.

CHAPTER SIX focuses on **moral teaching**. Catechesis teaches us how we are to live, as well as what we are to believe. This chapter explains how to live and act as disciples of Christ.

CHAPTER SEVEN explores the various **settings and circumstances** in which catechesis takes place. It deals with issues such as teaching the faith to people of diverse backgrounds, ages, and abilities who live and work in differing contexts and situations.

CHAPTER EIGHT focuses on **those who catechize**. Although catechesis is a responsibility shared by all the baptized, those such as bishops, priests, deacons, Catholic school teachers, and parish catechists have special roles.

CHAPTER NINE presents the ways in which catechetical efforts are organized and supervised, by both **dioceses and parishes**.

CHAPTER TEN focuses on **resources** for catechesis, including traditional materials such as books and other printed materials, as well as electronic and computer related materials.

FINALLY, the text concludes by entrusting the catechetical efforts of the United States to the **intercession of the Blessed Virgin Mary**, our national patron under the title of the Immaculate Conception.

Prayer to Mary, Star of Evangelization

O Blessed Virgin Mary,
we ask you who prayed to strengthen the faith of the first disciples
to obtain for the Church in the United States an outpouring of the Holy Spirit,
to guide us in a new evangelization.
Help us teach the faith in such a way that the members of the Church today
will truly be Christ's disciples of this new millennium
drawing people throughout the world to the saving message and power of Christ.
We ask this through Jesus Christ, your Son and our Lord. Amen

Mary, Star of Evangelization, pray for us.

Adapted from the *National Directory for Catechesis*, p. 302.

The document *National Directory for Catechesis Bulletin Insert* was developed as a resource by the Committee on Catechesis of the United States Conference of Catholic Bishops (USCCB). It was reviewed by the committee chairman, Archbishop Daniel M. Buechlein, OSB, and has been authorized for publication by the undersigned.

Msgr. William P. Fay
General Secretary, USCCB

Lord God,
source of all wisdom and knowledge,
you sent your Son, Jesus Christ, to live among us
and to proclaim his message of faith, hope, and love to all nations.

In your goodness
bless our brothers and sisters
who have offered themselves as catechists for our Church.
Strengthen them with your gifts
that they may teach by word and example
the truth which comes from you.

We ask this through Christ our Lord.

Amen.

Summary

of the

National

Directory

for Catechesis

COMMITTEE ON CATECHESIS
United States Conference of
Catholic Bishops

The *Summary of the "National Directory for Catechesis"* was developed as a resource by the Committee on Catechesis of the United States Conference of Catholic Bishops (USCCB). It was reviewed by the Committee on Catechesis, was approved by the committee chairman, Archbishop Daniel M. Buechlein, OSB, and has been authorized for publication by the undersigned.

Msgr. William P. Fay
General Secretary, USCCB

Contents

Introduction

TEXTUAL NOTE: This publication is a faithful summary of each chapter of the *National Directory for Catechesis*. It is designed to provide a brief survey of the text's content, not to replace the text itself, where principles and guidelines for catechetical instruction are presented in full.

The Second Vatican Council called for the renewal of catechesis. This call resulted in the promulgation of many significant universal Church documents: the *General Catechetical Directory* (1971), *Rite of Christian Initiation of Adults* (1972), Pope Paul VI's apostolic exhortation *On Evangelization in the Modern World* (1975), and Pope John Paul II's *On Catechesis in Our Time* (1979). Under the leadership of Pope John Paul II, who has zealously contributed to the renewal of catechesis in the contemporary Church, the *Catechism of the Catholic Church* (1992) and the *General Directory for Catechesis* (1997) together represent a synthesis of catechetical ministry for the universal church.

The documents intended for the whole Church have served as the inspiration and foundation for our own national catechetical directories: *Sharing the Light of Faith* (1979) and the new *National Directory for Catechesis* (2005), both of which are official documents of the United States Conference of Catholic Bishops. The *National Directory for Catechesis*, reviewed and approved by the Congregation for the Clergy in the Holy See, provides fundamental theological and pastoral principles, drawn from the Church's Magisterium, for the pastoral activity of catechesis in parishes and dioceses within the United States. The *National Directory for Catechesis* is intended primarily for those who have responsibility for catechesis in dioceses, parishes, and schools; but all those who participate in the Church's mission to proclaim the Gospel will find it useful. The *National Directory for Catechesis* is also a fundamental reference for authors, editors, and publishers of catechetical texts and other catechetical resources. The guidelines in the *National Directory for Catechesis*, which are aimed at the continued renewal of catechesis in the United States, set forth the nature, purpose, aims, tasks, basic content, and methodologies of catechesis.

Although some members of the Church are called to more specific catechetical roles, fostering growth in faith is the responsibility of the entire Christian community. The *National Directory for Catechesis* will be a source of hope and encouragement to all who participate, directly and indirectly, in catechetical ministry—deepening their reliance upon God, and helping them recognize how God, Father, Son, and Holy Spirit, works in and through them to bring the message of salvation to all.

1

Proclaiming the Gospel in the United States

Catechesis necessarily occurs within a social and cultural context.
Thus, catechists must consider the Christian message in relation to
the particular circumstances in which they announce it.

The Holy Spirit is the primary agent of evangelization, who makes possible the encounter between the Word of God and the many diverse languages and cultures throughout the world. In this context, the first chapter of the *National Directory for Catechesis* describes the cultural and religious factors that currently affect catechesis in the United States, discussed under four main headings: (1) general characteristics of U.S. culture, (2) diversity in U.S. culture, (3) a profile of Catholics in the United States, and (4) family and home in the United States.

General Characteristics of U.S. Culture

U.S. culture is marked, first and foremost, by great emphasis on *freedom*. This God-given right to freedom is in itself a positive value, underlying the pluralism and diversity for which the United States is known. However, many distortions of genuine freedom exist in our nation: most significantly, the exaggerated emphasis on an individual's freedom and rights. Such a distorted view of freedom can result in moral relativism and privatization of religion.

A second characteristic of U.S. culture is the value it places on *religious freedom*. The principle of separation of church and state holds that government must not establish a single religion as the religion of the state or prefer one religion over another. The government must also protect the free exercise of religion in all states.

This principle has enabled people of different faiths to find a home in America. However, the principle of religious freedom has also been construed as calling for the complete separation of religion from public life.

Economic freedom is a third quality important in U.S. culture. The principles of individual responsibility, equal opportunity, and the free enterprise system govern American economic freedom. While most agree that individuals should enjoy equal access to economic and social opportunities, a wide gap exists between rich and poor. Because of this gap, the Catholic faith upholds the need to judge economic decisions or institutions by the extent to which they protect human dignity and allow participation of all.

Pragmatism, a focus on practical rather than intellectual knowledge, is a fourth trait permeating U.S. culture. While a pragmatic orientation has positive aspects, pragmatism can also encourage a utilitarian attitude—that is, the idea that something has value only to the degree that it is concretely useful.

Developments in *science and technology* represent both blessing and challenge. Many of these developments promote the good of the whole human community. However, they also create the ability to produce unconscionable evil. The rapidity of these scientific advances often leads to situations in which the means to do something is discovered before the ramifications are given adequate consideration. The moral good or evil of developments cannot simply be based on some promised benefit of a particular technological development—the intrinsic nature of the means and the implications for the well-being of the human person and human community must also be assessed.

A worldwide force affecting U.S. culture is rapid *globalization*. In positive ways, globalization has led to higher standards of living for many. But a negative effect of globalization has been an increase in the already wide gap between rich and poor peoples and nations. The Gospel calls all to global responsibility and solidarity, which includes the protection of the poor and vulnerable in the United States and around the world. U.S. Catholics have a special responsibility to work toward solidarity, in part because the United States, more than any other nation, bears great responsibility for cultural and economic globalization.

Finally, *mobility* in the United States continues to shape its culture. Immigration, transportation, and communications technology have resulted in community life that is based more on affinity than on geographic or neighborhood contexts. This has a profound effect on parish life and catechesis. For example, many Catholics look for parishes and religious education programs where they can enjoy a strong sense of community—and do not automatically join those communities and programs that are geographically closest.

Diversity in U.S. Culture

The United States is marked by great cultural and religious diversity, representing nearly all ethnicities and religious traditions.

Diversity Within the Catholic Church

Catholics in the United States, representing 23 percent of the general population,[1] are a diverse mixture of races, ethnicities, and cultures. This cultural pluralism within the Church is a positive value, and the distinctive identities of each culture should be preserved even while unity of faith is promoted.

Many Eastern Catholic Churches are also active in the United States. Together, in communion with the pope, these Churches are a visible sign of the unity of the Church of Christ, and the resulting diversity of expression united in the one faith enriches the Church.

Regional Diversity

Each region of the United States has particular geography and demographics, and each also comprises various religious groups. The Northeast is dominated by mainline Protestant traditions and is also home to large numbers of Catholics; it is more secularized and urbanized than the Midwest and the South. In the South, evangelical Protestant faiths and other religious bodies play a special role in the culture. The Midwest combines aspects of the more secular Northeast and the more socially conservative and evangelical Protestant South. The West has the fewest inhabitants who indicate any affiliation with organized religion; in the Pacific Northwest in particular, anti-Catholicism is a reality.[2]

Profile of Catholics in the United States

The current population of Catholics in the United States is 62 million and growing, and the number of dioceses and eparchies has also grown. Parish life has generally increased in scale and complexity. Twenty-two percent of parishes celebrate Mass in languages other than English at least once a month, with Spanish being the second language in the vast majority of these parishes.[3]

At the same time, the number of parishes without full-time pastors has increased. The number of priests, both diocesan and religious, has not kept pace with the growth of the Catholic population. The number of Catholic parishes with schools has decreased, even as the number of young Catholics participating in parish-based religious education programs has grown.

In addition, the numbers of women and men religious have declined by half since the 1960s, and their average age is more than sixty-three years. Meanwhile, lay ministers have greatly increased in number. Some have pursued professional training and serve as parish and diocesan leaders in catechesis, Liturgy, and pastoral ministry. Many more serve as catechists, RCIA team members, liturgical ministers, youth ministers, social justice advocates, parish council and committee members, and ecumenical representatives.

Family and Home in the United States

Family and home life in the United States show positive trends, and policy makers have increasingly acknowledged the need to address family concerns in public policy. Yet negative elements also plague marriage and family life in the United States, and for Catholics in particular: high divorce rates, a high rate of cohabitation among those who come for marriage preparation, the decline of traditional nuclear families, and the increase of single-parent households.

Four trends underlie these social changes. First, respect for human life is challenged by the acceptance of abortion, the move toward physician-assisted suicide, and a pro-contraceptive mentality. Second, the essential bond between husband and wife is challenged by individualism. Third, the natural authority of parents over children is challenged by a distorted sense of self-sufficiency and autonomy. Finally, the transmission of traditional values within the family is challenged by popular culture and by the mobility of migrant families.

The Catholic Church offers an alternative to these forces by upholding its vision of marriage and family, reminding all of the importance of the family as the domestic church, and looking to the Trinity as the model of family life.

Notes

1   See Barry Kosim, Egon Mayer, and Ariela Keysar, *American Religious Identification Survey* (New York: Graduate Center of the City of New York, 2001), 12.

2   See Frank Hobbs and Nicole Stoops, *Demographic Trends in the Twentieth Century* (Washington, DC: U.S. Census Bureau, 2002); Edwin S. Gaustad and Philip L. Barlow, *The New Historical Atlas of Religion in America* (Oxford: Oxford University Press, 2001).

3   See *The Official Catholic Directory* (New Providence, NJ: P. J. Kenedy & Sons, 2002); Center for Applied Research in the Apostolate (CARA), *Special Report: National Parish Inventory* (NPI) (Washington, DC: CARA, 2000).

2

Catechesis Within the Church's Mission of Evangelization

The Church exists to evangelize. Evangelization expresses the Church's identity and completes the mission entrusted to her by her founder, Jesus Christ. Catechesis is a significant moment in the process of evangelization. Through comprehensive, systematic instruction and initiation into the life of the community through the Liturgy, sacraments, and service, catechesis deepens and strengthens the believer as a member of the Body of Christ, the Church.

Christ calls all members of the Church to proclaim Christ to every generation. Christians evangelize by professing faith in Christ, celebrating the Christian mysteries in the Liturgy, praying, and embracing the Christian way of life.

Catechesis is an important moment in the evangelizing mission of the Church. Catechesis echoes the word of God contained in Revelation, transmitted through Scripture and Tradition, and faithfully preserved in the teaching authority of the Church.

Revelation

Revelation is the act by which God manifests himself personally to us in order to share his divine life and to bring us into communion with him as the Father, Son, and Holy Spirit. In this way, God fulfills his plan of love for the salvation of the world and enables us, through the gift of faith, to respond to his invitation to know, love, and serve him.

God first revealed himself through creation, which he sustains and guides towards its perfect fulfillment.

History also discloses God's saving plan, particularly in the covenants God made with Israel when he formed them as a people. To fulfill the covenant with David, God promised to send a Messiah and establish his kingdom forever. Revelation reached perfect fulfillment when the Word became flesh in Mary's womb and dwelt among us. Jesus Christ completed and perfected Revelation through his words, deeds, signs, and wonders and, above all, by his death and Resurrection and the sending of the Holy Spirit to remain with his disciples forever.

God's Revelation, contained in Scripture and Tradition—commonly known as the "deposit of faith"—remains living and active in the Church today, safeguarded by the Magisterium.

Faith is a gift to us from God. It has two dimensions: the faith *by which* one believes and the faith *which* one believes. *By* faith, one personally adheres to God; *through* faith, one freely assents to the truth that God reveals and transmits through the Catholic Church.

Evangelization and the Ministry of the Word

All members of the Church are called to engage actively in a *new evangelization* of the world. Directed to members of the Catholic Church seeking to revitalize their faith and sacramental worship, the new evangelization entails motivating them toward permanently engaging in catechesis; toward integrating a truly Christian spirituality into the personal, political, economic, and social aspects of life; and toward acting in favor of social justice. The new evangelization is also directed to every member of the human family and to every dimension of contemporary culture: aiming to convert to Christ those who have not previously heard or understood the Gospel, moving them to explicitly confess faith in Jesus Christ and to open themselves to transformation in Christ.

Evangelization as a ministry of the Word is realized in four stages: (1) the proclamation of Christ to non-believers and the indifferent; (2) initial catechesis for new believers; (3) continuing catechesis to deepen and mature the faith of believers; and (4) pastoral ministry to those committed to Christ.

1. *Pre-evangelization*, the initial stage, ordinarily builds on the basic human needs of those to be evangelized: food, shelter, love, security, and acceptance. Then, the Word is announced in a way the hearers can understand: to members of other religious traditions, the religiously indifferent, non-believers, Christian children, Christians with minimal or deficient catechesis, and non-practicing Christians.

2. The next stage, *initiatory catechesis*, introduces catechumens, children, and those with minimal knowledge of the faith into the life of the Christian community. Through systematic instruction, prayer, initiation into sacramental life and worship, and involvement in pastoral activities of the local church, initiatory catechesis nurtures a new way of life in Christ.

3. Next, the aim of *post-baptismal catechesis* (mystagogy) is to extend and fortify the believers' relationship to Christ and the Church. Through reflection, instruction, and prayer, Christians are led to a deeper understanding of and active participation in liturgical worship and a life of charity and justice.

4. *Ongoing catechesis* deepens a believer's knowledge of Christ and the Church and helps to integrate the truths of the faith into all spheres of life: individual, family, social, economic, and political.

This catechesis can take place in a liturgical or educational setting. *Liturgical catechesis* aims to enrich and expand the meaning and impact of the sacraments in the lives of the individual and the Church. Reflection upon sacramental signs, symbols, and rituals deepens and enhances the celebration of the Liturgy, especially the Eucharist. *Theological catechesis* systematically explores and investigates the truths of the faith in dialogue with philosophy and the social sciences. It aims to make the proclamation of the Gospel meaningful to contemporary men and women and to motivate ongoing conversion to a Christian way of life.

The context for evangelization in the United States is rich and diverse. Creative methods, consistent efforts, and flexible catechetical programs are required to address negative aspects of cultural pluralism, such as moral relativism, religious indifference, alienation from institutional religion, or marginal association with the Church. The contemporary situation in our nation demands ongoing catechesis for all members of the Church, to ensure continuing conversion to a Christian way of life so that we may live by values compatible with the Gospel and reject those contrary to it.

Source and Sources of Catechesis

The source of catechesis is the Word of God revealed by Jesus Christ. All catechesis draws its content from this living source, transmitted in Scripture and Tradition. Together, they make the revelation of Christ present, active, and fruitful in the Church.

Other sources of catechesis include liturgical worship, reflection on the word of God and the lives of the saints, prayer and actions promoting social justice, the study of theology, and the daily witness of an authentic Christian life.

Nature and Purpose of Catechesis

The aim of catechesis is to lead believers to a deeper knowledge and love of Christ and the Church and a firm commitment to follow him. Jesus Christ is at the heart of all catechesis. It is in communion with Jesus that all believers share in the mystery of the Holy Trinity—the Father, the Son, and the Holy Spirit.

Catechesis is an action of the Church and is intimately bound with the whole of the Church's life. Catechesis shapes the initial proclamation of the Gospel. It prepares for the celebration of the sacraments, facilitates integration into the ecclesial community, urges apostolic activity and missionary witness, instills a zeal for the unity of Christians, and prepares one for the ecumenical understanding and mission of the Church. The Church is the origin, locus, and goal of catechesis.

The Tasks of Catechesis

Jesus formed his disciples into a community of faith. He instructed them, prayed with them, showed them how to live, and entrusted to them the mysteries of the Kingdom of heaven. After his death and Resurrection, he sent them the Holy Spirit and commissioned them to go out and teach all nations. The fundamental task of catechesis is, therefore, to form disciples of Christ and to send them forth in mission. Following the example of Jesus the Teacher, catechesis encompasses six diverse yet interlocking tasks, as described by the *General Directory for Catechesis*:

1. Catechesis promotes knowledge of the faith.
2. Catechesis promotes meaningful participation in liturgical worship and the sacramental life of the Church.
3. Catechesis integrates moral formation into a Christian way of life.
4. Catechesis teaches Christians how to pray with Christ, in Christ, and in communion with the Church.
5. Catechesis initiates the Christian into the life of the local church community and fosters active participation in the mission of the Church.
6. Catechesis promotes a missionary spirit that prepares Christians to witness to Christ in society.

These six tasks of catechesis constitute a unified whole. While each task realizes the goal of catechesis, all of the tasks are interdependent. For catechesis to be effective, no task should be separated from the rest.

Inculturation of the Gospel Message

God's Word became flesh in Jesus Christ, a particular man born into a specific time and culture. The Incarnation of the Son of God is the divine model for inculturation and evangelization.

Every culture has the potential to welcome the gospel message proclaimed by the Church through the ages. To be effective, evangelization requires the inculturation of the gospel message. Inculturation is an interactive process that listens for echoes of the word of God in a particular culture and discerns values and practices compatible with the Gospel, purifying those that are incompatible and rejecting anything hostile to the Gospel.

In the multicultural, pluralistic social context of the United States, effective catechesis is *inculturated* catechesis, in which catechetical activity seeks to

- Discover the seeds of the Gospel present in a culture
- Respect the culture of those to whom the Gospel is addressed
- Appreciate that the gospel message transcends the limitations of human culture
- Proclaim the transforming good the Gospel can bring about in every culture
- Promote a new enthusiasm for the Gospel
- Adopt linguistic and cultural expressions that foster the transmission and reception of the gospel message
- Express coherently and convincingly the content of the faith without compromise

The catechist performs a vital role in this process. By interpreting the gospel message faithfully and communicating it understandably in the idiom of the local culture, the catechist enhances the reception of the mysteries of Christ entrusted to the Church.

3

This Is Our Faith; This Is the Faith of the Church

The content of faith is the heritage of the whole Church. It is the privilege and responsibility of the entire people of God to preserve the memory of Christ's words and actions and to hand on the content of this faith to future generations.

The faith that we have received has come down to us from the Apostles. In handing on the faith that Jesus entrusted to them, the Apostles and their successors made use of short summaries or creeds that synthesized the Christian faith and were intended for catechesis, especially for candidates for Baptism. The *Catechism of the Catholic Church* is a catechesis of the Creed. Chapter 3 in the *National Directory for Catechesis* offers an introduction to the Catechism and its use in catechetical ministry.

The Symphony of the Faith

Sacred Scripture, the *Catechism of the Catholic Church*, the *General Directory for Catechesis*, and the *National Directory for Catechesis* are distinct yet harmonious instruments for the Church's catechetical ministry.

In every age of the Church, the study of Sacred Scripture has been the cornerstone of catechesis. Frequent, direct use should be made of the biblical texts themselves, and the Gospels should be presented so as to foster a relationship with Christ. The *Catechism of the Catholic Church* is a statement of the Church's faith and of Catholic doctrine, attested to or illumined by Sacred Scripture, Apostolic Tradition, and the Church's Magisterium. It is a sure and reliable reference for teaching the faith. The *Catechism* is structured around four fundamental dimensions of the Christian life: the profession of faith, the celebration of the Liturgy, Christian moral life, and prayer.

Criteria for Authentic Presentation of the Christian Message

The word of God found in Sacred Scripture and Sacred Tradition is the single source for handing on the Christian message. The presentation of the Christian message centers on the person of Jesus Christ. Every aspect of catechesis promotes following Jesus Christ. The Gospels are central to the catechetical message. They are the word of God, written by human authors inspired by the Holy Spirit.

Always Trinitarian, catechesis emphasizes the Trinity as the central mystery of Christian life. God as revealed by Jesus, the Incarnate Word, is Father, Son, and Holy Spirit. All Revelation has a Trinitarian character, and the goal of catechesis is to lead all to share in the Trinitarian communion.

Catechesis must proclaim the Good News of salvation in Jesus Christ. This salvation includes a message of liberation: liberation from all forms of sin, both personal and social. Through catechesis we come to understand that Christ inaugurated the Kingdom of God—of which the Church is the seed, the beginning.

In and through the Church, we can experience aspects of the Kingdom here on earth and receive a foretaste of the eternal Kingdom of heaven.

Because the faith that is handed on is the faith of the Church, catechesis is always an ecclesial endeavor. The faith of the Church has come to us from Christ through the Apostles, recorded in the Scriptures, celebrated in the Liturgy, and manifested both in the teachings of the Magisterium and in the witness of faithful women and men through the ages. Catechesis originates in the Church's confession of faith and leads to the believer's profession of faith.

The ecclesial character of the Christian message reflects its historic nature and the Church's role in carrying on the Lord's mission. Jesus Christ is a historical figure who preached the Good News of the coming of the Reign of God in time. He established the Church to continue both his presence and his mission in every generation. This Church continues, in word and sacrament, to make present Christ in a way that enables his wisdom and teaching to be applied to the circumstances of our day and to interpret present events of human history.

The inculturation of the Gospel is a key criterion for the pastoral presentation of the Christian message. Since the ecclesial community is the principal setting for inculturation, the parish must prepare catechists in their native language and cultural situation; use culturally appropriate catechetical methods, tools, texts, and resources; foster catechetical leadership that reflects the cultural diversity; and attend to the popular devotions and feasts common to the various cultural groups within the parish.

Catechesis must also recognize and teach the hierarchical character of the Christian message. The mystery of the Most Holy Trinity is the central mystery of Christian faith and life and is therefore the most fundamental and essential of all teaching. While all the truths of faith form an organic or harmonious unity, other truths are organized around these fundamental truths: the Trinity, the Incarnation, the presence and work of the Holy Spirit, and the mystery of the Church as the Body of Christ.

The final criterion for the presentation of the Christian message is that it should foster a common language of faith so that the faith may be proclaimed, celebrated, lived, and prayed in words familiar to all the faithful. The biblical language and the formulas of faith are important because of the realities they express and the identity they foster. The contemporary relevance of traditional formulas should be explained in language suited to the people and culture being addressed.

4

Divine and
Human Methodology

The transmission of the gospel message continues to be a work of the Trinity. By God's grace, some people are called to proclaim the Gospel as catechists. Whatever human methods these catechists employ must be based on the model of God's own methodology—the Father's self-revelation in Jesus Christ and through the Holy Spirit.

Always a concern, methodology entails attention not only to the organization of content but also to age and ability and to the language and culture of the group being catechized. The paradigm for contemporary methodology derives from the pedagogy of God, which engages persons and communities in light of their circumstances and their capacity to accept and interpret Revelation, God's self-communication in Jesus through the Spirit.

God's Own Methodology

Through God's self-disclosure of the loving communion of Father, Son, and Holy Spirit, he makes known the mystery of his divine plan and its ultimate purpose—the salvation of the human person. This plan is realized gradually through God's actions and words. The way God has revealed himself to us serves as a source and model for all pedagogy of faith.

The Pedagogy of God

Since God is one God in three Divine Persons, the work of Revelation and salvation is the work of the whole Trinity. But Tradition atttributes primary agency for certain activities to each of the three Persons in accordance with their inner relation to one another.

God the Father

Through the mystery of the Incarnation, Jesus revealed God as his Father and as the Creator of all that exists. God the Father has revealed himself in other ways to people of faith in generation after generation—ways that included a covenant with his people and the Law given to Moses to help God's people live lives of faithfulness. God the Father has acted in human history in many ways and is made manifest most fully in his Son, Jesus.

Jesus Christ

As the Word of God made flesh, Jesus Christ is the sacrament of God and the preeminent model for the communication of faith and the formation of believers. The way Jesus related to his disciples as well as to the crowds whom he addressed reveals God's own methodology as the model for all catechetical methods. Jesus often began with an experience familiar to his listeners, questioned their assumptions, and finally challenged them to make a decision. His methodology was multidimensional and included words, signs, and the wonders that he worked.

The Holy Spirit

The action of the Holy Spirit in the Church continues the pedagogy of God. With Christ, the Holy Spirit animates the Church and directs her mission. The Holy Spirit makes new life in Christ possible by manifesting the Risen Lord to believers. He also opens the minds of believers to an understanding of Jesus' death and Resurrection so that they may accept the Paschal Mystery as the paradigm of their own lives.

The Church

Under the guidance of the Holy Spirit, the Church continues to catechize her members in a way that reflects and relies upon God's own methodology.

Catechesis and Divine Methodology

Catechesis as communication of divine Revelation conveys God's loving plan of salvation in the person of Jesus Christ. Building on God's own methodology, genuine catechesis

- Emphasizes God's loving initiative and the person's free response
- Accepts the progressive nature of Revelation, the transcendent and mysterious nature of the word of God, and the word's adaptation to different persons and cultures
- Recognizes the centrality of Jesus Christ
- Values the community experience of faith
- Is rooted in interpersonal relations and employs the process of dialogue
- Utilizes signs that link words and deeds, teaching and experience, and especially visible signs that express and make present the invisible reality of God's presence
- Draws from the Holy Spirit its power of truth and a commitment to bear witness to the truth

Elements of Human Methodology

The communication of faith in catechesis is, first, an event of grace under the action of the Holy Spirit, realized in the encounter of the word of God with the experience of the person. In handing on the faith, the Church does not rely on any single method. Many circumstances have to be considered, including the age and ability of the learner. Whatever the method, there should be interaction and harmony—and no opposition—between the content of faith and the method.

Catechetical methods use two basic approaches: inductive and deductive. Inductive methods begin with the experience of the learner and lead to divine truth. Deductive methods begin with the truths of faith and apply them to the concrete experience of the person. Distinct yet complementary methods for communicating the faith, both are legitimate approaches when properly applied. That is, the deductive method has full value only when the inductive method is properly utilized.

Learning takes place in many ways:

- *Human experience*, a constitutive element in catechesis, provides a starting point that must be linked to the revealed word of God in order to help people explore, interpret, and judge their basic experiences in the light of the Gospel. Human experience provides the sensible signs that lead the person by the grace of the Holy Spirit to understand the truths of the faith and the profound questions in life.
- *Learning by discipleship* is an integral element in catechesis because Christian discipleship means following Jesus Christ in one's own time, place, and circumstance.
- The witness of the *Christian community* is an important element in catechetical methodology. The effectiveness of catechesis will depend upon the vitality of the parish and the extent to which it is a clear, living, and authentic sacrament of Christ. Catechesis is the responsibility of every member of the Church.
- The *Christian family and home* ordinarily provide the most formative environment for growth in faith. It is within the Christian family that members are awakened to the presence of God and learn to pray and to form their consciences in light of the teachings of Christ and of the Church. Children learn by the selfless witness of their parents and other family members.
- The *witness of the catechist*, under the guidance of the Holy Spirit, powerfully influences

those being catechized through faithful proclamation of the Gospel and the example of the catechist's life. They must firmly believe in the Gospel and its power to transform as well as live the Gospel in their own lives.

- *Learning by heart*, or memorization, is a constitutive aspect of the pedagogy of faith because it fosters a common language of faith and an identity among all the faithful. Basic prayers, creeds, key biblical themes, important figures of faith, and aspects of worship and the Christian life are memorized in order to encourage the individual to participate in what is being taught and to relate it to the whole of the Christian life. Learning by heart should continue to have a special place in catechesis today.

- *Learning by Christian living* is an essential component of catechetical methodology. Generally, the faithful can learn as they respond to God's initiative through praying, celebrating the Liturgy and sacraments, living the Christian life, fostering works of charity and of justice, addressing injustices that exist in the systemic and institutional organization of society, and promoting virtues such as liberty, solidarity, justice, peace, and protection of the environment.

- *Learning by apprenticeship* links an experienced Christian believer or mentor with one who seeks a deeper relationship with Christ and the Church. An example of learning by apprenticeship is the relationship that often develops between a catechist and a catechumen. The aim is to promote an authentic following of Christ based on the acceptance of one's baptismal responsibilities, the internalization of the word of God, and transformation to life in Christ.

Means of Communication

Much of what we know and think about today is conditioned by the various means of mass communication. For this reason, the effective use of media is essential for evangelization and catechesis. All media should be used to proclaim the gospel message. Catechists must seriously commit to learning how to use these means of communication in order to bring people to Christ. However, they must also develop a critical ability to recognize the ways in which the media promote messages contrary to gospel values.

5

Catechesis in a Worshiping Community

In the Liturgy, the Church both expresses faith and, through the grace of God, deepens that faith. Gathered to worship the Father in Christ and through the Holy Spirit, the Church becomes more aware of her mission to the world.

Faith and worship are closely related: faith gathers the community for worship, and worship renews the faith of the community. In the Liturgy, the official public worship of the Church, the Church celebrates what she professes and lives: above all, the Paschal Mystery by which Christ accomplished the work of our salvation. Chapter 5 of the *National Directory for Catechesis* describes liturgical catechesis for the sacraments and the liturgical year, as well as sacramentals, popular piety, and devotions.

Relationship Between Catechesis and Liturgy

Catechesis both precedes the Liturgy and flows from it. Liturgical catechesis helps people to fully, consciously, and actively participate in the Liturgy. It also helps them to reflect on the liturgical actions, to discern the implications of their own participation, and to respond by witness and service. Liturgical catechesis promotes a more informed knowledge and deeper understanding of the meaning of the Liturgy and sacraments.

Liturgical and Personal Prayer

Prayer nurtures our vital and personal relationship with the living and true God. Personal prayer is God's initiative, and the response to that gift is prompted by the grace of the Holy Spirit. Personal prayer and liturgical prayer are both part of the life of the Church. Because catechesis seeks to lead individuals and communities to deeper faith, catechesis for prayer emphasizes the primary aims of prayer—adoration, thanksgiving and praise, petition, and contrition—and includes various prayer forms: communal, private, traditional, or spontaneous; gestures, songs, meditation, and contemplation. Catechesis for prayer begins when children see and hear others praying and when they pray with others, especially in the family.

Catechesis for Sacraments in General

The liturgical life of the Church revolves around the seven sacraments, with central emphasis on the Eucharist. Fundamental principles apply to catechesis for each of the sacraments. Catechesis for a sacrament should

- Present a comprehensive and systematic formation in the faith, one that integrates knowledge of the faith with living the faith
- Center on initiation into the life of the Triune God, and present Christian life as a lifelong journey
- Be appropriate to the age level, maturity, circumstances, language, and ethnic background of those being catechized

- Be directed to all members of the Christian community, and be offered within and through the whole community of faith
- Involve parents in the formation of their children
- Be integrated into the total catechetical program
- Focus primarily on the symbols, rituals, and prayers contained in the rite for each sacrament
- Enable the believer to reflect on the meaning of the sacrament received by implementing a thorough experience of mystagogia following the celebration

Official catechetical norms, guidelines, and other essential tools for catechesis on the sacraments are found in the *General Instruction on the Roman Missal* and in each of the specific rites. Other resources to be consulted are *Rite of Christian Initiation of Adults*, *Guidelines for the Celebration of the Sacraments with Persons with Disabilities*, the *Directory for Masses with Children*, the *Directory for the Application of Principles and Norms on Ecumenism*, and the *Directory on Popular Piety and the Liturgy*. (See the resource list at the end of this publication.)

The baptismal catechumenate is the source of inspiration for all catechesis. The formation has four stages: pre-catechumenate, catechumenate, purification and enlightenment that prepares for the reception of the Sacraments of Initiation, and post-baptismal catechesis (mystagogy). This process is an inspiration for the lifelong formation of the whole community. Catechesis takes place within the community through instruction and the celebration of liturgical rites for the purpose of living as disciples of Christ.

The fourth period, mystagogy, in the broadest sense represents the Christian's lifelong formation in faith. Lifelong catechesis takes many forms, including participation in the Eucharist and study of the Liturgy, study of the Sacred Scripture and Catholic social teachings, reflection on life events in the light of faith, and opportunities for prayer, spiritual exercises, and acts of charity.

Catechesis for Particular Sacraments

Christian initiation is celebrated in Baptism, Confirmation, and Eucharist. Through these Sacraments of Initiation, believers are drawn into the communion of the Holy Trinity. They become partakers of God's own life, are incorporated into the Body of Christ, and are strengthened for discipleship by the Holy Spirit.

God intended that all people be saved by Christ's self-sacrificial love. For this reason, Christ founded his Church to continue his work of healing and salvation through the power of the Holy Spirit. Christ cured many who were sick, exorcized demons, and forgave sins. His healing ministry is carried on in the Church primarily through the Sacrament of Penance and Reconciliation and the Sacrament of the Anointing of the Sick.

The eternal plan of God the Father for the salvation of all people is further realized by Christ through the Holy Spirit, in the Church, in the Sacraments of Holy Orders and Matrimony. These Sacraments at the Service of Communion contribute to the life of the Church, the Body of Christ.

Chapter 5 of the *National Directory for Catechesis* lists specific catechetical guidelines proper to each sacrament.

The Sacred: Time (Liturgical Year) and Space (Art)

The Paschal Mystery, the mystery of salvation through Jesus Christ, lies at the heart of the liturgical year, a cycle of feasts and seasons. Throughout the year, the Church celebrates this Paschal Mystery every Sunday, the day of the Lord's Resurrection. The liturgical year unfolds in a way that corresponds to the major events in the history of salvation in Christ. The Christmas season celebrates the mystery of the Incarnation. The Easter season recalls the mystery of redemption. Each is preceded by a preparatory season: the Christmas season by Advent, and the Easter season by Lent.

The weeks of the year not part of either Advent and the Christmas season or Lent and the Easter season are designated as Ordinary Time. During this time, the Church celebrates different aspects of the fullness of the mystery of Christ from week to week.

In the course of the liturgical year, the Church also honors Mary, the Mother of God and Mother of the Church under many titles. The lives of apostles, martyrs, and saints are also commemorated. The unfolding of the liturgical year offers constant opportunities for catechesis.

Sacred art, architecture, and music also serve a catechetical purpose. Sacred art is essential to the Church at prayer because it expresses the divine presence. The church building is a sign and reminder of the immanence and transcendence of God. Sacred music gives glory and praise to God and forms an integral part of the Liturgy; especially for the parts of the Mass, sacred music also enriches the people's active participation in the Liturgy. It also has a catechetical purpose: to invite the people to give glory to God, foster the unity of their minds and hearts, and draw them closer to Christ.

Sacramentals and Popular Devotions

Sacramentals are instituted by the Church in order to sanctify the lives of the faithful. They can involve the blessing of certain ministries in the Church such as catechists or lectors, certain states of life such as members of consecrated life, and certain objects such as church buildings, holy water, rosaries, or ashes. Catechesis on sacramentals should describe their relationship to faith in Christ and their function in the Church and in the lives of individuals.

Especially in light of the cultural, ethnic, and religious diversity of the United States, popular piety is a vital element in Catholic life, expressed in a variety of ways. As a mode of inculturation of the faith that is deeply rooted in the cultures represented, popular piety and devotions provide opportunities to encounter Christ in the particular circumstances of ethnic, cultural, and religious customs. Catechesis must give careful attention to the role of popular piety in the lives of people, especially in the lives of new immigrants. Devotion to the Blessed Virgin Mary deserves special attention because it is such an important part of worship in the United States among many different cultures.

Care must be taken to ensure that popular devotions enrich the Church's sacramental life but do not replace it. All devotions should also lead the faithful to a deeper sense of their membership in the Church.

6

Catechesis for Life in Christ

Catechesis for life in Christ seeks to inspire individuals and communities to allow life in Christ to be the vital principle of all their activity.

The Christian moral life entails living the call to holiness through transformation in Christ. The discipleship to which Christ has called all believers demands love and self-surrender. Catechesis for life in Christ is a catechesis of the Holy Spirit, the interior guide; a catechesis of grace, the love of God; a catechesis of the Commandments, of the Beatitudes, of sin and forgiveness, of human virtues, and of the twofold commandment of charity. This catechesis always begins and ends in Christ. Chapter 6 of the *National Directory for Catechesis* describes the catechetical principles and guidelines needed for personal and social moral formation, as well as the witness that is to be given to the new life in Christ by individuals and by the community of faith.

The Dignity of the Human Person

All Christian moral life is rooted in the dignity derived from God's creation of us in his image and likeness. This divine image is present in every person. In Christ God reveals how human beings are to live. God created us with freedom: every person is a free and responsible agent with the right to exercise that human freedom, the capacity to choose good or evil. The more one chooses to do what is good, the more one becomes free. The choice to do evil is an abuse of freedom.

Secular culture often contradicts Christian values and threatens the dignity of every human being.

Abortion and euthanasia directly attack innocent life; biological and technological developments can undermine human dignity. The treatment of people such as immigrants or undocumented persons, or of criminals and their victims, must be shaped by the awareness of the inherent dignity of every human person. In a culture in which freedom often means individual autonomy and personal choice, the individual person is pitted against society and social life, and even family life is emptied of its significance. Secularism, materialism, and ethical relativism erode moral reference points and thereby diminish people's ability to make moral decisions.

To address challenges to the dignity of the human person, catechesis on Christian morality must

- Uphold the right to life from conception to natural death
- Present the distinctly Christian understanding of human freedom
- Teach that freedom reaches its authentic goal in love of the weak and the defenseless and in defense of their rights
- Promote the public contribution of the Christian faith to public policy
- Encourage concern for the lives of the poor, the weak, the disabled, and the sick, as well as action on their behalf
- Help the faithful to make practical moral decisions in the light of the Gospel

- Encourage the faithful to understand that power, wealth, and productivity must be subordinate to and guided by higher moral values

Moral Formation in Christ

Christian moral formation involves conversion to Christ, including confession of faith, adherence to his person and teaching, and faithful discipleship. Divine grace transforms human nature so that a person can lead a morally good life. Virtue is the habit of tending toward the good and choosing the good in the concrete actions of a person's life. The theological virtues of faith, hope, and charity—the foundation of Christian moral living—transform the human capacity to do good into a participation in divine nature.

The formation of a moral conscience has to be rooted in the individual's relationship with Christ. Moral conscience is a judgment of reason whereby the human person recognizes the morality of a concrete act. It bears witness to the truth and judges particular choices, decisions, and actions to be either good or evil. Because the conscience can make erroneous judgments, people are responsible for ensuring that their consciences are well formed and that their actions reflect God's law, which is written on their hearts.

To communicate fundamental moral teachings, catechesis should restore a sense of the sacred and transcendent in life, to enable people to understand that God shares his own life with them and sustains them with his unfailing love. Catechesis helps people to form their consciences and make concrete moral judgments—to identify and recognize the effects of sin, an offense against God that turns the human heart away from his love. Sin wounds human nature and injures human solidarity.

Catechesis seeks to enable people to recognize and obey the divine law, based on universal truth and revealed by God, and to grow in virtue and commit themselves to a deep personal relationship with Christ.

The Human Community

The model for the human community is the Holy Trinity, the unity of Father, Son, and Holy Spirit. The very nature of the Trinity is communal and social. We who are made in God's image share this communal, social nature and are called to build relationships of love and justice. Christian morality has a distinctly social dimension that derives from the nature of the human person and the Church's social mission. Followers of Christ have the responsibility to apply Christian values to social systems, structures, and institutions in an effort to root out injustice. The Church's social teaching is a living tradition of thought and action, a framework that includes the totality of Christ's moral teachings and those proposed by the Church in his name.

The Church's emphasis on the social dimension of morality has led to the development of the concept of social sin, that is, personal sin expressed in the structures of society with social implications. Sinful structures contribute to social relationships that cause systematic denial or abuse of the rights of certain groups or individuals. Organized social injustice, institutionalized racism, systemic economic exploitation, and widespread destruction of the environment are examples of the social consequences of sin. Despite the difficulties in eradicating these evils, individuals are moral agents and need to work with others to change those structures and systems that cause evil.

Moral Formation in the Gospel Message

The Church has the responsibility to form its members in light of the Gospel and to teach them how to apply Christian moral principles to contemporary problems in specific and practical ways. The Ten Commandments (Decalogue) and the Beatitudes are the primary reference points for the application of Christian moral principles. The Decalogue expresses God's covenant with his people and is a privileged expression of the natural law that sums up love of God and neighbor. The Beatitudes teach the attributes and virtues to be cultivated in those who follow Jesus.

Other teachings of the Church that provide moral principles for Christian life are found in the Spiritual and Corporal Works of Mercy, the Theological Virtues and moral virtues, the seven capital sins, and the Precepts of the Church. Sacred Scripture and the lives of the saints provide concrete positive examples of Christian moral living. Those being catechized should not only know the Ten Commandments and the Beatitudes by heart but also understand how the teaching of the Beatitudes was already implicit in the Decalogue. In general, catechesis should present the teaching of the *Catechism of the Catholic Church* on the Decalogue in light of Christ's teaching in the Sermon on the Mount. Chapter 6 of the *National Directory* *for Catechesis* presents guidelines for each of the Commandments in order to assist the catechist in presenting the meaning of the Commandments and Beatitudes in a comprehensive and authentic manner.

7

Catechizing the People of God in Diverse Settings

The Church's catechesis presents the universal truth of the Gospel to every stratum of human society, in a wide variety of catechetical settings, in an effort to transform society and renew the face of the earth. In this catechesis, the Church recognizes and celebrates diversity within the community of faith, affirms the fundamental equality of every person, and acknowledges the need for charity, mutual respect, and justice among all groups in a pluralistic society in ushering in the Kingdom of God.

Teaching was central to the ministry of Jesus. He was sent by the Father to proclaim the coming of the Kingdom of God and to draw humanity into communion with the life of the Holy Trinity. For two thousand years the Church has taken up Christ's command to go, make disciples, and teach. The Church is both the principal agent of catechesis and the primary recipient of catechesis. Every individual has the responsibility to grow in faith and to contribute to the faith of the other members of the Church. For this endeavor, the Church must take serious account of the circumstances and cultures in which the faithful live in order to present the meaning of the Gospel in an understandable way. Chapter 7 of the *National Directory for Catechesis* offers principles, guidelines, and criteria for presenting the Gospel to different groups in their diverse settings.

Catechesis According to Readiness and Age Levels

Growth in faith is related to human development and its stages.

Adult catechesis should be the foundation that gives coherence to catechesis for all ages, from children to the elderly. The goals of adult formation—conversion, participation in the Christian community, and discipleship—serve as the umbrella for all other forms of catechesis. The content of adult catechesis is directed toward discipleship developed through doctrine, celebration, moral formation, prayer, community participation, and missionary spirit. (A full treatment of the content of adult catechesis is found in *Our Hearts Were Burning Within Us*.) Methodology for adult catechesis varies, but this catechesis is always a basic, organic formation in the faith that includes a serious study of Christian doctrine integrated with formation in Christian living.

The *National Directory for Catechesis* offers specific guidelines for catechesis of other age levels.

The catechesis of *elderly* people is most effective within the context of a comprehensive program of pastoral care. Often, the elderly themselves are the most effective catechists for their peers and therefore need to be given the same opportunities for formation that are provided to all catechists.

Young adults should receive special consideration as they search for meaning in their lives, during a time in which they are often making important life decisions. As they face the challenges of many negative influences of society, they are vulnerable to feeling apathy, cynicism, and indifference to God and the Church. Catechesis for young adults should take place within the context of comprehensive pastoral care that addresses the questions they ask and recognizes the problems they face.

Significant physical and emotional changes characterize the period of *pre-adolescence and adolescence*. Just as with young adults, the most effective catechetical programs combine catechesis, community life, evangelization, justice and service, leadership development, pastoral care, prayer, and worship. Two areas of special concern are catechesis for the Sacrament of Confirmation and catechesis for Christian vocation.

The formation of *infants and children* begins in the home. Although it is generally informal, unstructured, and spontaneous, early formation is crucial to the child's development in faith. Structured catechesis begins in catechetical programs suited to the age, circumstances, and learning ability of children and is designed to reinforce the Christian values found in the family. The school and parish, through the witness of adults, provide an environment in which young people can grow in faith. At this age level, catechesis is gradual and systematic, integrating knowledge of the faith, liturgical life, moral formation, prayer, community life, and a missionary spirit.

Catechesis for Persons with Disabilities

Persons with disabilities are integral members of the Christian community and should be welcomed into ordinary catechetical programs as much as possible. Catechesis for some persons with disabilities, however, can require more personal attention or special access services (such as sign language interpretation) to meet specific needs. For those with developmental disabilities, involvement of families or other caretakers is essential because they are a resource for understanding the needs of the individual.

Catechesis in Special Situations

The community of the baptized comprises many different groups of believers, each of whom has the right to adequate catechesis. Special groups may include professional people, the marginalized, the socially and economically disadvantaged, college students, military personnel, unwed parents, married couples, homosexual persons, the divorced or widowed, and males or females. As much as possible, catechesis should be developed in consultation with those for whom it is intended so that it can better help them respond to God's uniquely personal love for each of them within the context of their special situation.

Catechesis in the Context of Ecumenical and Interreligious Dialogue

Catechesis helps to form a genuine ecumenical attitude in those being catechized. In order to engage in authentic ecumenical work, Catholics must know their own tradition well enough to be able to present the doctrine of the Church clearly and unambiguously, in a considerate manner that honestly presents the differences but avoids placing obstacles to dialogue. Catholics must likewise present the teachings of other churches and religions correctly and honestly, taking care not to misrepresent them. Catechesis must teach Catholics to respect the faith of others.

While ecumenical formation is necessary for all the Christian faithful, catechists in particular must have a firm grasp of basic Catholic principles of ecumenism. The *Directory for the Application of Principles and Norms on Ecumenism* is a resource for ecumenical formation of catechists. (See resource list for information about obtaining a copy.)

Special care should be given to catechesis in relation to Judaism, seeking to foster a correct and fundamental understanding of its history and traditions. Catechists must take care to affirm the value of the whole Bible and to appreciate the special meaning of the Old Testament for the Jewish people. Catechesis should teach both the independence and the interconnectedness of the Old and New Testament, emphasize the Jewishness of Jesus and his teachings, and show that Christians and Jews together consider the Ten Commandments to be a foundation of morality.

Catechesis in relation to other non-Christian religions has distinctive characteristics. Catholics need to be familiar with the history of Islam and its beliefs in order to work for mutual understanding. Catechists must be well informed not only about Islam but also about other non-Christian religions in order to promote respectful relationships with all peoples. Because the United States includes many new religious and spiritual movements, sects, and cults, catechesis in relation to New Age movements should accurately describe their tenets and carefully contrast them with Catholic beliefs and practices. The proliferation of these new movements reveals a hunger among many to find transcendent meaning in their lives. Christians need to reach out to others, offering the Gospel and the richness of our Christian spiritual tradition, which responds to the deepest longings of the human heart.

8

Those Who Catechize

Catechesis takes place in the many settings and all levels that make up the Church: family, parish, diocese, and nation. Catechists are called from a wide variety of backgrounds and talents. These catechists and these settings reflect life in the Holy Spirit. Nourished by prayer, the celebration of the Eucharist, and the building of community, they make catechesis ring true in the hearts and minds of those to whom the catechist is sent.

Although all members of the community of believers in Jesus Christ participate in the Church's catechetical mission, Chapter 8 of the *National Directory for Catechesis* focuses on the roles and responsibilities of those who are called to more specific catechetical roles and provides principles, guidelines, and criteria for their formation as catechists.

Differing Roles of Those Who Catechize

Since the proclamation and transmission of the Gospel are central to the episcopal ministry, the *bishop* has primary responsibility for catechesis in the diocese. The bishop sees that the ministry throughout his diocese is supported by competent personnel, effective means, and adequate financial resources. He must also ensure that the catechetical materials used in the diocese transmit the faith completely and authentically. The bishop might consider designating a diocesan director and staff to aid him in this work.

Since *pastors* are the bishop's closest collaborators in ensuring that the goals of the diocesan catechetical mission are achieved, they have a special responsibility. Pastors need to ensure that catechesis is provided for the parish celebration of the sacraments and that the parish offers ongoing, age-appropriate catechetical formation.

Priests, *parochial vicars*, *deacons*, and *seminarians*, in collaboration with the pastor, have the responsibility of forming the Christian community and fostering the ministry of catechesis by providing catechists with training and support. The parish priest should play an active role in the catechetical program, being available to celebrate the sacraments with classes or groups and assisting catechists in carrying out their responsibilities. In order to enrich their ministry as catechists, priests and deacons need to give careful attention to their own catechetical formation. Seminarians need a clear understanding of the nature, goals, and methods of catechesis as well as the processes of human growth, development, and faith formation to prepare for their future ministry as parish catechetical leaders.

By virtue of their vocation, *those in consecrated life* catechize by the witness of their vocation and their apostolic work. Throughout the history of the Church, religious have committed themselves to catechetical ministry and are particularly suited to serve as parish or diocesan catechetical leaders.

The single most critical factor in an effective parish catechetical program is the leadership of a *professionally trained parish catechetical leader* who works under the direction of the pastor. Parishes must allocate essential resources to obtain a competent and able parish catechetical leader. *Coordinators of youth ministry* need theological formation as well as competence and experience in catechesis. Dioceses should provide training for youth ministers as well as catechists in general, including a certification program when possible.

While all members of academic communities have the opportunity to build up the Church on the university and college campus, the *campus minister* has a unique and important role. Campus ministry provides catechesis to students, faculty, and staff alike.

The Catholic school not only provides academic instruction of high quality but is also an effective means for Christian formation. Under the direction of the pastor or school board, the *principal* plays a critical role in meeting the catechetical objectives of the parish. In order for the Catholic school, as a center for evangelization, to have a distinctly Catholic identity and character, a catechetical program must be an essential part of the school. *Religion teachers* must have a thorough knowledge of the Christian message and the ability to communicate it. They also need to give personal witness to the truth of what they teach. The Catholic school is a particularly favorable setting for catechesis because it provides daily opportunities for proclaiming and living the gospel message.

Parents and guardians, as well as *families*, are the most influential agents of catechesis for their children. They catechize primarily by the witness of their Christian lives and by their love for the faith. Parents or guardians are catechists for their children precisely because they are parents or guardians, not because they have developed any specialized skills. When children are baptized, parents accept the responsibility to bring up their children in the practice of the faith. At the same time the Church promises to help parents foster their children's faith. Parish life with its celebration of the Liturgy, vibrancy of the community, adult catechesis, the parish school, and catechetical programs for children and preparation for sacraments is an aid to parents and guardians.

Preparation and Ongoing Formation of Catechists

In the Church's catechetical ministry, many catechists are volunteers who bring a wide variety of talents and abilities to the vocation of catechist. The call to be a catechist is not arbitrary but is instead a process of discernment involving the catechist, pastor, and parish catechetical leaders. When the pastor invites an individual to become a catechist, some form of commissioning ceremony should be held (preferably on Catechetical Sunday, typically held in September) to express the Church's call and the catechist's generous response. Those who have a specific ministry to catechize should strive to develop their human and spiritual qualities as well as their catechetical skills. The *National Directory for Catechesis* offers guidelines for catechetical formation, both in the initiatory stage and in the ongoing formation of the intellectual, spiritual, and apostolic life of catechists.

The formation of catechists takes place most effectively within the local parish. Parish-centered programs remind the catechists that their call comes from the Church, that they are sent by the Church, and that they hand on the faith of the Church. Parish-centered programs offer opportunities for the formation of a local community of prayer, mutual support, and learning.

Opportunities for catechist formation are also provided by the diocese. The development of comprehensive catechist certification programs, institutes, workshops, and seminars are within the purview of the diocese. Some dioceses work closely with Catholic colleges or universities to set up training and certification programs. Productive use of distance-learning models can be another means of assistance for dioceses and parishes.

9

Organizing Catechetical Ministry

The presentation of the Gospel requires the best efforts of the Church at every level and the tireless dedication of the entire community of the faithful. National, regional, diocesan, and parish catechetical structures embody Christ's apostolic commission—to go and make disciples, baptize, and teach—through practical forms, functions, organizations, policies, and procedures. These are essential if the Church is to be faithful to her mission in the world.

Within catechetical ministry is a diversity and complementarity of responsibilities, as well as the need for coordination of those involved in catechesis. Chapter 9 of the *National Directory for Catechesis* offers principles and guidelines for the development of a comprehensive pastoral plan at the parish, diocesan, and national level.

General Principles and Guidance

- Organization at the parish, diocesan, and national levels should be part of an overall pastoral plan that comes from the church's comprehensive mission.

- Organization for catechesis is person-centered, with particular support for the family as the basic community, and encourages participation of all the catechized in determining organizational structures.

- The goals of catechesis, accountability, and channels of communication should be clearly stated.

- Organizations should ensure equitable distribution of services, resources, and opportunities. Parishes in need should have opportunities equal to those of more affluent parishes.

- Essential aspects of catechetical organizational planning are analysis of the diocesan situation, assessment of needs and resources, identification and prioritization of goals and strategies, establishment of a realistic budget and overall working plan for the catechetical mission, and periodic review and evaluation.

Diocesan Structures

In the diocese, the referent point for the organization of catechetical pastoral care is the bishop and the diocese itself. The bishop has the final responsibility for a catechetical plan and its success. He may consult with a variety of bodies, such as various diocesan councils, in establishing and implementing a catechetical plan. The bishop relies on a diocesan catechetical director, through which he can direct and moderate the catechetical activities of the diocese. Since catechesis is an integral part of other diocesan offices, collaboration among the different agencies is imperative.

The Parish Community

The parish is the preeminent setting for the catechesis of adults, youth, and children. Like the diocese, every parish needs to develop a coherent catechetical plan. Sometimes this is done through a catechetical committee or commission that helps to plan, coordinate, and implement various catechetical activities within the parish. The members of the committee or commission should represent the diverse age, ethnic, social, and economic backgrounds present in the parish.

Some Pastoral Efforts

Comprehensive parish-based catechesis harmonizes all segments of the parish so as to allow a realistic opportunity to grow in understanding and practice of the Catholic faith. Careful consideration can also be given to the possibility of cooperating in *extra-parochial* or *inter-parochial efforts*. Smaller neighboring parishes might consider combining catechetical programs and personnel, especially if a single pastor is shared by two parishes.

Within the parish catechetical plan, priority should be given to *adult catechesis*, allocating funds for programs and for the personnel, time, and space needed for programs in adult faith formation. Other pastoral efforts in parishes can focus on *family-centered programs* that can help strengthen the bonds of the family, particularly interchurch families. Parents who choose to catechize their children at home are part of the parish's total catechetical effort. They need to be supported and guided in a curriculum approved by the diocesan bishop, need to be encouraged to fully participate in the life of the local parish, and need to attend appropriate training sessions provided by the parish or diocese.

All parishes provide *catechesis for children of all ages*, whether they attend Catholic or public schools or are home-schooled. Effective organization of parish catechetical programs for children should include enthusiastic evangelization and recruitment efforts to reach families whose children do not participate in parish activities.

Catholic schools, vital to the church's mission of evangelization and catechesis, are an integral part of the total parish catechetical plan. The Catholic school should strive to integrate the Catholic faith into every aspect of its life, seeking to relate all human culture to the Gospel so that the life of faith will illuminate all knowledge that is part of the school curriculum.

Youth catechesis is yet another aspect of the Church's catechetical mission. It is most effective when situated within a comprehensive program of youth ministry that includes social, liturgical, and catechetical components as well as opportunities for service.

The *baptismal catechumenate* is a vital component in the organization of catechesis in the parish and should be the cornerstone of the parish catechetical plan. The catechetical plan of the parish also needs to include a process of initiation for candidates for full communion who are already baptized. This process should respect the particular circumstances, experience, knowledge, and Christian practice of each individual.

Small Christian communities, found in many parishes, are important centers for the development of Christian virtues and human values. They often provide the faithful with an experience of a more intense community life. Since small Christian communities provide a natural setting for adult faith formation, the catechesis offered in these communities should be consistent with other elements of the parish catechetical plan.

While the parish remains the primary setting for catechesis, *other structures are beyond the boundaries of a single parish*. For example, some Catholic schools are regional or private schools not connected to a single parish. Other examples include catechetical programs for persons with disabilities, daycare and after-school programs, convalescent and nursing homes, residential facilities for persons with physical, mental, or emotional disabilities, and other organizations outside the parish but under church auspices—all of which should have a catechetical dimension.

Regional and National Associations

The formation of the faithful involved in a number of professional groups, movements, and associations that provide opportunities for religious devotion and apostolic service should always include catechesis. All of these organizations are to be integrated into the diocesan catechetical plan, in collaboration and communication with the diocesan bishop and local pastors. Dioceses also need to be aware of and to make use of information and resources provided by independent national organizations and associations.

The Service of the United States Conference of Catholic Bishops (USCCB) and of the Holy See

The USCCB has established a standing Committee on Catechesis within its permanent structure and has provided personnel and resources for its effective operation. The purpose of this committee is to serve the bishops in addressing the catechetical needs of the country as a whole.

The USCCB works closely with the Congregation for the Clergy, which assists the Roman Pontiff in the exercise of his ministry to proclaim and hand on the Gospel of Jesus Christ to the ends of the earth.

10

Resources for Catechesis

Catechetical aids that are faithful to God's Revelation of the truth in Jesus Christ and suited to the particular needs of those to be catechized can be very effective in the hands of skilled catechists. These materials should reflect fidelity to authentic doctrine with adaptation to specific circumstances.

No catechetical materials, resources, or tools—no matter how excellent—can replace the catechist. But sound catechetical resources in the hands of faithful and skilled catechists can be powerful instruments in proclaiming the Gospel and fostering growth in faith. Catechetical resources are many and varied: Sacred Scripture, the Church's official documents and catechisms, catechetical textbooks and other instructional materials, multimedia resources, and various means of telecommunications technology. Chapter 10 of the *National Directory for Catechesis* provides specific principles, guidelines, and criteria for developing, producing, selecting, evaluating, and using these materials.

Resources in General

The preeminent source for evangelization and catechesis is Sacred Scripture. Catechesis should make frequent, direct use of biblical texts and should present the Gospels in a way that elicits an encounter with Christ.

The *Catechism of the Catholic Church* is the authoritative contemporary expression of the living Tradition of the Church and a re-presentation of the deposit of faith in today's world. This basic resource for all catechetical activity provides a reliable guide for instruction and formation in Christian faith and life. One of the primary aims of the *Catechism of the Catholic Church* is to assist the bishops and the Chris-

tian people in the preparation of local catechisms. Local catechisms are invaluable because they take into account various situations and cultures, while preserving the unity of faith and catholic doctrine. A local catechism always requires the approval of the Holy See, which recognizes the catechism as a text of the universal Church that has been prepared for a specific culture and situation.

Catechetical Textbooks and Other Instructional Materials

In the United States, catechetical textbooks for children and youth are ordinarily part of an integrated series that has been prepared for a number of grade or age levels. Materials for adults often take the form of adult catechisms or resources for the baptismal catechumenate, for parish renewal, and for small Christian communities. Catechist and teacher manuals are essential components of a sound catechetical textbook series. Other instructional materials includes parent education material, resources for the baptismal catechumenate, and additional sacramental materials that enrich knowledge of the curriculum. Supplementary materials should be well integrated into a basic textbook series, in conformity with the *Catechism of the Catholic Church* when possible, and be artistically sensitive, technically up-to-date, theologically authentic, ecumenically accurate, and methodologically sound.

Communications Technology and Catechesis

Television has made a dominant impact on the education and formation of children. Consequently, the use of media is now essential in evangelization and catechesis. Contemporary communications media, however, do not merely transmit information; they generate visual, audible, emotional, and, in some cases, entirely virtual experiences for individuals and communities. Well-planned catechesis must employ these media so that the message of Jesus Christ can be effectively communicated in the real circumstances and culture of those who seek him.

Media take many forms, including print, audiovisual, and electronic materials. It is important that catechists receive training in the use of media, including the specific characteristics of different media, ways to distinguish between reality and virtual reality, ways to identify the primary and secondary messages communicated, and opportunities to become proficient in the use of the equipment. A parish or diocesan plan should include instruction on how to evaluate the media messages in light of the Gospel. An awareness of the techniques used by advertisers to influence and manipulate is critical, as is the ability to distinguish between the image presented and the reality or the distortion of reality that it represents. Viewers must understand the profit motives of commercial television and the Internet.

Preparation and Evaluation of Catechetical Materials

All catechetical textbooks and other materials are to be prepared according to the criteria and guidelines contained in the *National Directory for Catechesis*. General guides are the *Catechism of the Catholic Church* and the *General Directory for Catechesis*. In particular, authors, editors, and publishers should adhere to the guidelines for the preparation of catechetical resources in *Guidelines for Doctrinally Sound Catechetical Materials*. A further refinement of that document is found in the *Protocol for Assessing the Conformity of Catechetical Materials with the Catechism of the Catholic Church*. The fundamental criteria for guiding the development of catechetical materials derive from the principles of authenticity and completeness.

The preparation of catechetical materials should also be based on sound principles of catechetical methodology and take into account the cultural, racial, and ethnic diversity of those who use the materials.

The local bishop makes the determination about which catechetical materials may be used in a particular diocese. The bishop should establish a process for evaluating catechetical material, assessing both the doctrine presented and the methods used and taking into account the foundational documents, the diverse communities, and consideration of the overall diocesan catechetical plan. The bishop might call upon his diocesan catechetical staff to coordinate this evaluation process, inviting a representative group of pastors, principals, parish catechetical leaders, teachers, catechists, and parents to serve on a catechetical material selection and evaluation committee.

Conclusion

The *National Directory for Catechesis* provides the fundamental theological and pastoral principles drawn from the Church's teaching and offers guidelines for applying these principles within the catechetical mission of the Church in the United States. The *National Directory for Catechesis* was developed by the bishops of the United States to be a source of inspiration for a new evangelization and for a renewed catechesis in the dioceses and parishes of this country. This renewal should lead those who seek Christ to know him ever more deeply and to bear courageous witness to him in an increasingly secular world. It will only reach this goal insofar as it is a renewal in the Holy Spirit by the Holy Spirit.

May the Virgin Mary, whose intercession was once responsible for strengthening the faith of the first disciples, obtain for the Church in the United States the outpouring of the Holy Spirit, as she once did for the early Church. This gift will then make present the new evangelization and revitalized catechesis to which Christ's disciples of the new millennium will be his powerful witnesses.

Resources

Papal Documents

John Paul II, *On Catechesis in Our Time (Catechesi Tradendae)*. 1979. Washington, DC: USCCB.

Paul VI, *On Evangelization in the Modern World (Evangelii Nuntiandi)*. 1975. Washington, DC: USCCB.

Vatican Documents

Catechism of the Catholic Church, 2nd. ed. 2000. Washington, DC: USCCB–Libreria Editrice Vaticana.

Directory for the Application of Principles and Norms on Ecumenism. 1993. By the Pontifical Council for Promoting Christian Unity. Washington, DC: USCCB.

Directory for Masses with Children. 1973. By the Sacred Congregation for Divine Worship. In *The Liturgy Documents*, volume 1, 4th ed. (pp. 291-304). Chicago: Liturgy Training Publications, 2004.

Directory on Popular Piety and the Liturgy: Principles and Guidelines. 2002. By the Congregation for Divine Worship and the Discipline of the Sacraments. Available at http://www.vatican.va/roman_curia/congregations/ccdds/ documents/rc_con_ccdds_doc_20020513_vers-direttorio_en.html

General Catechetical Directory. 1971. By the Sacred Congregation for the Clergy. Available at http://www.vatican.va/roman_curia/congregations/cclergy/documents/rc_con_cclergy_doc_11041971_gcat_en.html

General Directory for Catechesis (GDC). 1998. By the Congregation for the Clergy. Washington, DC: USCCB.

USCCB Documents

General Instruction of the Roman Missal (GIRM). 2001. By the International Commission on English in the Liturgy (ICEL) and the USCCB. Washington, DC: USCCB.

Guidelines for the Celebration of the Sacraments with Persons with Disabilities. 1995. By the USCCB. Washington, DC: USCCB.

National Directory for Catechesis (NDC). 2005. By the USCCB. Washington, DC: USCCB.

Our Hearts Were Burning Within Us: A Pastoral Plan for Adult Faith Formation in the United States. 1999. By the USCCB. Washington, DC: USCCB.

Rite of Christian Initiation of Adults (RCIA). 1988. By ICEL and the USCCB Bishops' Committee on the Liturgy. Washington, DC: USCCB.

Sharing the Light of Faith: National Catechetical Directory for Catholics of the United States. 1977. By the USCCB. Washington, DC: USCCB.